SETTING

MEN

FREE

SETTING
MEN
FREE

by
BRUCE LARSON
Author of *Dare to Live Now!*
and *Living on the Growing Edge*
Editor of *Marriage Is for Living*

ZONDERVAN PUBLISHING HOUSE
GRAND RAPIDS, MICHIGAN

Since God has used Bruce Larson so powerfully in my own life to help me find freedom, I can really recommend his new book, *Setting Men Free,* with much gratitude. Here is a clear, direct distillation of living experience. It is filled with sound help for laymen and ministers who want to bring Christ's renewal into their own lives, and the lives of those around them. I certainly recommend this book.

KEITH MILLER
Author of *A Taste of New Wine*

This book is dedicated to my wife,
HAZEL MARIE,
without whose love, correction, en-
·couragement, and editorial help this
book would not have been written;
and because God keeps using her
to help set me free.

CONTENTS

CONTENTS

INTRODUCTION

As I read this book, a flood of memories swept over me: memories of things recent, of more remote occurrences, of friendly faces, of encounters, of events similar to those the author tells about in *Setting Men Free*. Above all I recalled that most decisive period in my life, well over thirty years ago, when I suddenly discovered in a personal way those utterly simple yet fundamental and living truths which the reader will find in this book. Bruce Larson's request that I write an Introduction must have been prompted by the feeling that he and I are brothers, born of the same spiritual family and trained in the same school of practical and living Christianity. I share that feeling with him.

Writing this gives me the opportunity to acknowledge my debt to America, and to pay particular homage to a friend for whom both Pastor Larson and I had a deep reverence: Sam Shoemaker. Neither my wife nor I will ever forget the times we met with Pastor Shoemaker and his wife. Well remembered, too, are the experiences of that period and the resulting transformation of our lives.

To be sure, I was then already a Christian, and had been very active in church endeavors. But at that time *theory* outran *practice*, if I may put it that way. I was more adept at discussing religious issues than at leading men to Christ.

More than you Americans, we Europeans are given to abstraction and complexity. For this reason we need you badly. We delight in intellectual debate and in subtle arguments. Granted these have some value, nevertheless they are more limited to theologians, while our task as laymen is to live our personal communion with Christ with such intensity as to make it contagious.

The mere exhortation that I move from theory to practice would not have been effectual for me at that time. It took an inner movement to bring this about, a *prodding* which is born of precisely one thing: personal dialogue. I was not aware that though my Christian belief was sincere, I was in no way a free man since I had never in utter confidence bared to anyone my problems, my difficulties, or my most intimate compunctions. Therefore I may say that I am one more example to be cited along with all the others to whom Pastor Larson refers. I too took the steps to where I could hear God, could discover freedom, solidarity, the personal encounter with Jesus Christ and with my neighbor, and could come to know the art of living.

All this changed my own life and my relations with family and friends. It opened before me avenues of ministry in understanding my fellow men and in spreading the Gospel among them. It even began to condition my relationships with patients.

Anyone who is free — or, rather, on his way to freedom, for perfect freedom is never achieved — becomes available to his fellow men, who sense this availability and spontaneously open their hearts. So it was with many patients who began to talk to me in intimate detail. This was a novel experience and at first a very distressing one, for I had some qualms. I felt this was not the practice of medicine but something akin to the priesthood. "Come back this evening," I would say to a patient of long standing, "and we can talk by the fireside — not as doctor and patient but as one man to another."

For some time I lived two distinct but parallel lives. By day I was a medical practitioner like any other: probing, sounding, prescribing, operating; at night I ventured upon the strange and fascinating dialogue which Bruce Larson describes. Only after several years was I compelled to admit that this adventure in dialogue was in fact *very much* the practice of medicine, for it sought to remedy one of the gravest ills of our time: loneliness. On a par with any other medical technique, it contributed to the physical and psychological cure of the sick. Note that I say "contributed," for while unexpected cures may sometimes follow upon a patient's experience of Christ, upon surrendering to Him and to the impetus of the Holy Spirit, honesty demands that we admit such direct cures are quite rare.

On the other hand, the experience of Christ never fails to change the patient's mental outlook, his attitude toward his illness, his personal discipline, and his co-operativeness with the doctor. All of this gives greater efficacy to the classic techniques of medical and psychological care, when the patient actively works toward his recovery.

The second of my two parallel lives has little by little

preëmpted the first, for no one on earth can encompass all things in his grasp at once. Tremendous joys have been mine in this Christian dialogue, but great hardships, too, and many defeats. This is unavoidable. Jesus Himself faced the defeat of the Cross after saying that the disciple cannot be greater than the Master.

But then, as we see how complicated and obscure are the problems which human beings bring to us, and how obdurately they resist human solution, we run the risk of falling back into subtlety, intellectualism, and complexity. Earlier I spoke of these as great obstacles to a living Christian experience. So we must rediscover that single-mindedness of you Americans, and your burning zeal in helping others. Our principal need is for that challenge to our faith, as found in a book like this.

Indeed, faith is not shelter against difficulties, but belief in the face of all contradictions. My hope is that those who read this book will boldly pick up the gauntlet which God casts down before them through the author.

PAUL TOURNIER

Geneva, Switzerland
November 3, 1966

FOREWORD

Today every phase of man's life and endeavor is changing at an incomprehensible rate. Science, industry, world politics, social patterns, space exploration, communication, transportation, education, and many other areas are going through a revolution.

But nothing is more exciting than what is happening in the Christian Church in our time. God is raising up a lay ministry which is causing an upheaval in the Church comparable to the Copernican revolution (when scientists discovered that the earth revolved around the sun and not vice versa).

In this book I have attempted, first of all, to report on some of the instances of the emerging lay ministry in the lives of many people in a variety of situations, and to encourage the laity in many churches to discover God's power for an effective ministry. I hope also that the book will provide some guidelines and principles for participation in this amazing lay movement.

The title comes from the words of Jesus: "If the Son makes you free, you will be free indeed" (John 8:36). Christians are discovering a style of life in Christ that is not at all "religious" in the traditional sense but which abounds with freedom tempered by responsibility.

These pages should indicate something of the nature of this authentic style of life, marked by joy and freedom and effectiveness, to which our Lord calls us.

God the Creator acts uniquely in every encounter. Therefore this book is in no sense an attempt to reduce God's creativity to rigid steps or methods. But a glance at the chapter titles will reveal the approach. Five chapters indicate some of the primary gifts that God gives to His people for ministry. These have to do with the quality of our lives. After all, it is what we are rather than what we do or say which communicates life most effectively.

The other five chapters deal with basic skills which God can give through His Holy Spirit to help us to be effective ministers. Jesus said, "Follow me, and I will make you fishers of men" (Matthew 4:18). We are rediscovering the person-to-person ministry which has always been essential to God's plan for every man's life.

Since in a large measure this book is a report on what I have seen God doing in the lives of innumerable people, I am indebted to each of these companions of The Way. I am also indebted to many writers in the fields of theology and psychology, as well as in other areas, and my special thanks go to the many participants in the fellowship of Faith at Work, stretching around the world and representing almost every denomination. More specific thanks go to the staff of Faith at Work who have given tremendous encouragement, correction, inspiration, and editorial help. And, finally, I am indebted to my family, the greatest laboratory any of us has for encountering truth.

Foreword

As you read this book, you will soon discover, with the writer, that God is raising up secular saints for today's society. This is The Great Adventure of our time.

BRUCE LARSON

Faith at Work
279 Fifth Avenue
New York, N.Y. 10016

PART I

1. THE ART OF LIVING

WHAT DOES IT MEAN to live as a Christian?

At a dinner party I heard a dedicated public health nurse from Canada tell about her work among the Eskimos. She said that before the arrival of the white man these people had not had serious mental or emotional trouble, but now they were experiencing anxiety neuroses.

A doctor next to me exploded joyfully, "That's wonderful! It's about time they joined the human race!"

Though a little stunned, we soon realized what the doctor meant. There's far more to living than the avoidance of problems. Sometimes it's only in problems that we discover what it really means to be alive. Jesus said that He came that we might have life (John 10:10). The art of living He offers is far more than Biblical knowledge, a hope for the future, or freedom from problems. It is a life of fulfillment, involvement, direction, and sacrifice here and now.

God gives me many insights while I ride on the commuter bus daily from my home in New Jersey to New

York City. One day when I wanted to get some work done during the trip I took a seat over the wheel, hoping that no one would sit next to me, and spread my briefcase and papers on the adjoining seat.

At the last stop before expressing into New York, the seat beside me was the only one unoccupied. Two people got on the bus: a well-dressed young man and an elderly woman, and the young man beat her to the seat.

For several minutes I sat fiercely resenting this young man next to me. But being a Christian means that God deals with our resentments, and I began to lose mine in my concern and compassion for the woman, who was having a difficult time staying afoot as the bus lurched about.

I began to pray that someone would give her a seat. It was unthinkable that I should give up mine because I had work to do and one cannot work standing up on a bus. Before long, however, the Lord let me know that I was sitting on the answer to my prayer, and that I had better trade my irrelevant prayer for some relevant action. I offered the woman my seat. Then as I stood in the aisle, my focus was once again on the young man sitting just beneath me. In the midst of feeling smug about being both a gentleman and a Christian, I realized that my motives were all wrong and that I had to ask God to put a new and a right spirit within me.

Here was a lesson for me in microcosm. In a short space of time I had moved from (1) resentment, to (2) concern, to (3) irrelevant prayer, to (4) relevant action, to (5) relevant action with the right spirit. I realized again that to live as a Christian means to live under the lordship of Christ in a dynamic that may change with every situation.

Jesus Christ came to give us *life*. Sometimes we think that the salvation he brings has something to do with "religion," but *salvation* is just another word for *wholeness*. Christ came to make people whole, physically as well as mentally and spiritually. Sad to say, there are many committed Christians who are sick emotionally and who have experienced only a small part of salvation, while there are pagans who have amazing psychic health but who have no direction or purpose. In fact, they've missed the very center of life.

As Christians we must be concerned that we both receive wholeness and help others to receive it. In our ministry to others we must be aware of the ingredients of wholeness. When a doctor examines a sick person, he tries to make a simple, on-the-spot diagnosis, though at times a more complex examination with expensive laboratory equipment is required. But let us consider the simple, on-the-spot diagnosis of a physician: he checks respiration and pulse, skin tone, the color of the eyes, and, if the patient is conscious, whether he has been eating and eliminating normally. Even this cursory examination provides some clues to the nature of the illness.

We meet people in need every day, and as Christians we should know how to diagnose a person's need and how to bring relevant help.

When the Apostle Paul told his story before King Agrippa, the king at one point said, "Paul, are you trying to convert me?" Paul replied, "O king, I wish you were just like me — except for these chains." Paul certainly did not mean he was perfect, for he was acutely aware of his own needs, but he *had* discovered the art of living as a Christian.

In his book, *The Church Inside Out*,° the Dutch theologian J. C. Hoekendijk mentions three Greek words which describe the three aspects of the Kingdom of God which are the basis of the Christian style of life. The first is *kerygma*, the essential proclamation that God came among us in Jesus Christ, that He died for our sins, rose from the dead, and is now Lord of all of life. The second is *koinonia*, or fellowship in depth with a few other Christians. The third is *diakonia*, or service to people in the world.

In my own experience, these three seem precisely the ingredients for wholeness of life for an individual, for a group, or for a church. Many Christians have heard the *kerygma*, and they may even be in a small group fellowship in depth; but they are not in any kind of relevant and sacrificial service to others. On the other hand, some people are involved deeply in service and occasionally in fellowship, but they have never responded totally to the proclamation in terms of personal commitment. As we discover wholeness in a combination of these three ingredients, we can minister effectively to others.

Let us put these three elements into everyday language.

First, the response to the proclamation means that at some point we have by an act of will turned the man-

° Philadelphia: Westminster Press, 1966.

agement of our lives over to Jesus Christ. This can be done with great emotion or with none. It is the kind of decision required for marriage, for signing a lease on a house, or for making a will. We are not made perfect by it, but we begin a dynamic relationship, growing in awareness of ourselves and of Christ's demands on us.

A New York business executive found himself after a job change still dissatisfied in his new job. At a conference he met a number of people who had responded to the proclamation about Jesus Christ, and he decided to begin this Christian style of life. After one day back at the office he told his wife a great change had taken place in him. He no longer saw people as things to use (i.e., to buy from and sell to), but as persons with needs, whom he should love and to whom he should offer the gifts of his friendship, concern, and help.

The second element, koinonia, *means living in depth fellowship with a few other Christians.* One comes into this experience through initial openness with another person. We cannot say that we love God, whom we have not seen, if we do not love our brother whom we have seen (I John 4:20). To love truly is to become vulnerable, even as God so loved that He gave His Son to the world. To be vulnerable before another may mean being totally known by that person. The Scripture just referred to implies that if among all the people we have met there is no one person whom we can love totally — that is with whom we can be vulnerable — we cannot say that we love God.

The art of Christian living requires continual openness and honesty with a few "significant others," and transparency before the world. To live this way tests how much we believe God truly accepts us as we are. I once saw a tugboat in the Hudson River pumping bilge at a furious rate. I thought surely the boat would sink until I realized there was no danger of that provided the bilge pump kept ahead of the leakage. To be in depth fellowship is to live with others honestly, claiming forgiveness and newness. The Christian style of life is much more a tugboat pumping bilge than it is a tight ship without leaks.

Diakonia, *the third ingredient of wholeness, means entering into service to the world.* This service has no strings. We do not serve people in order to convince them of spiritual truth but rather because Christ loves them whether they know it or not. For His sake we bring cups of cold water or food or bandages, or we identify with them in their struggle for freedom. We're called to serve not only individuals but groups, for individuals are bound by the structures of the society in which they live. At times this service certainly involves a spiritual ministry, but it must also involve a ministry to men's physical and economic and political needs.

When the disciples of John the Baptist questioned Jesus' authority, He called attention to *physical* and *social* credentials: "Tell John . . . the blind receive their sight, the lame walk, lepers are cleansed, and the deaf hear . . . the poor have good news preached to them" (Luke 7:22). Many Christians have never discovered the third element of wholeness — this sacrificial ministry to others.

It has rightly been pointed out that the Christian

Church does not need to send its people into society, for they are already there. We need to discover how to serve people where we actually live and work.

The secular existentialist Jean-Paul Sartre says in his book, *Nausea*, "I find that I am alive and it sickens me." The Christian answer to this is neither a shallow optimism nor a dour cynicism. Rather, it is to see life as it is and to discover the wholeness that is possible in Christ.

A major turning point in my own life came five years after my act of personal commitment to Christ, when I dared to be honest with another person about my needs as far as I saw them. This was a devastating experience, but it led to freedom and a new kind of effectiveness. Ever since that time I have sought out a few people in each town where we have lived with whom mutual honesty, openness, and commitment are possible. Some Christians are incisive in asking others to give their lives to Christ, but they do not think of the important next step: challenging them to enter into openness with a few other Christians.

Jesus Christ has not called us simply to go out and "be good," but to live life with Him. A close friend of mine identified with the proper young writer in *Zorba, the Greek*, who seems to be an observer rather than a participant in the game of life. Finally the writer turns to the morally uninhibited, middle-aged Zorba, who knows how to live exuberantly, and says to him, "Teach me to dance."

The Gospel is good news! The Lord has turned our mourning into dancing (Psalm 30:11)! Too often people feel they must make the empty choice between an inhibited morality and an exuberant immorality. But Christians should be confronting their lost and lonely contemporaries, most certainly with a moral message, but also certainly with an *exuberant* morality. Jesus Christ says, "I came that you might have life and have it more abundantly."

2. THE ART OF CONVERSATION

JESUS WAS THE GREAT conversationalist. We often think of Him as the great physician or the great teacher, but in many of His encounters with people He had no such credentials. Yet the Bible indicates that He began countless ordinary conversations, with amazing results. We have the same opportunity for meaningful conversation in everyday life — on the bus, in the office, at school, in the supermarket.

Many Christians feel they could be more effective with people if they were clergymen, Bible experts, or church officers. But unlike counseling, which takes place between an *expert* and a *seeker*, conversation takes place between *equals*. Some of today's inspired psychologists find that the most meaningful relationships are often established when they meet people as equals rather than on a "professional" basis.

To have dialogue with a gifted Christian conversationalist is a rare and wonderful experience. I will always be thankful for a conversation I had with such a person. He listened to me. He was interested in my struggles, doubts, and hopes. He seemed to understand me. He shared some of the concerns of his own life which were very much like my own. From time to time he asked questions. Finally he prayed with me, not in a condescending way but as a fellow seeker trying to discover God's best. I came away from that conversation a different person.

I am convinced that God intends all Christians to be effective conversationalists. Perhaps this is the highest expression of "the priesthood of all believers." People are eager for love and acceptance. Through the art of conversation we can demonstrate that God knows them, loves them, and understands them.

When Jesus spoke with the immoral woman by the Samaritan well, an entire town was affected. She ran into her village announcing that she'd met a man who had told her all there was to know about herself. She did not say this man had raised the dead, or healed the sick, or taught great truths. Yet the town came running en masse to meet Him.

Jesus tells us that the things He did we shall do also. The ability to understand people is one of the most effective gifts any Christian can have in the service of his Lord.

Let us begin with some general suggestions which can help us to understand people.

First of all, take no one for granted. A person is like an iceberg: one tenth shows and the rest is submerged.

There is a true story about a man who parked his car in front of a supermarket. When he returned, he found the front of his car smashed and no sign of the offending car. His heart sank until he noticed a scrap of paper tucked under the windshield wiper. Opening it, he found this message: "As I am writing this note to you, there are at least sixteen people watching me. They think I am giving you my name and address. Well, I'm not." The point is clear: very often the *obvious* is not the *actual*.

People will begin a conversation with trivial things — things which are not threatening. As they trust us more, they may mention the problems of a husband or wife, a child or friend. All the while they may be hoping that we will get at the deeper problems of their own behavior.

Psychology textbooks, especially those in the field of psychosomatic medicine, give interesting clues to "reading people." For example, it is said that the person who constantly picks at his cuticles is trying to destroy himself. The woman who raves about how wonderful and perfect her husband is really hates him. People suffering from backache often complain that someone "gives them a pain." The person with chronic migraine headaches frequently mentions "blowing his top." In point of fact, each of us is an open book for the discerning to read. The way we dress . . . the way we talk . . . the things we say . . . the things we don't say . . . our eyes, our posture, even our skin tone: all of these reveal what we are, what we think and feel, and what has happened to us.

We need not consult books on psychology to learn how to recognize revealing signs in people around us. The gift of reading men comes primarily through listening and observing with a lack of self-consciousness. If we cannot read others, perhaps it is because we attach too much importance to making the right impression, or we feel the need to be loved, admired, or respected. The person who has been justified by faith does not need to impress men or gain their approval. If we believe that God loves us and accepts us as we are, we can begin to relate to people unself-consciously.

Understanding ourselves is essential to understanding others. As we begin to know our own motives and fears, hopes and anxieties, in some measure we know all men. We differ in surface traits, but in depth we are much alike.

One of my friends from seminary days had the ability to read people because he knew himself. One night I listened as Bill talked about the Christian life with a graduate student of foreign affairs. For over an hour this student did an expert job of refuting every one of Bill's arguments about the reality of God, the person of Christ, and the purpose of life. Finally Bill laughed and said, "Why don't you admit that you really are lonely, afraid, and defeated?" The graduate student was stunned. "How did you know?" he asked. I am sure he thought Bill was clairvoyant. But Bill knew himself and therefore knew his friend and was able to pierce his defenses. Several weeks later the graduate student made a commitment of his life to Jesus Christ.

Try to determine the particular way in which God is working in each man's life. For a helpful conversation, understanding man's nature and needs in general is not enough. Everyone we meet has had some experience of God, whether he knows it or not, and everyone we meet, even the most sincere Christian, still has a "growing edge" where God is at work bringing maturity. As we enter into conversation, we must discern where God is already at work and what He has already accomplished. Two good questions to ask ourselves are: *What does this person have?* and *What does he lack?* Let me give three examples to illustrate what I mean.

(1) A beautiful young mother, a church member, had been addicted to alcohol and drugs for years. She had had shock treatment and psychiatric therapy to no avail. The turning point came while she was recovering from delirium tremens in a psychiatric ward. Her minister visited her and said, "Mary, you're going to be all right. God loves you and is working in your life. *Believe that.*" She did believe it. She joined Alcoholic Anonymous and is now helping others to find a new life.

(2) A corporation president living in suburbia, a moral, honest man but not a Christian, lost his job in a merger and with it his sense of identity and purpose. He came close to a nervous breakdown and began to visit a psychiatrist. The lively Christian couple next door were having conversations with him during this difficult time, and at one point they said, "How marvelous that you have lost your job. Now you can find out who you really are and can find God's plan for your life." He committed his life to Christ and discovered that as a child of God, his identity was not contingent on his job, and that his purpose was more than making money for stockholders and for himself. Incidentally, he now has a new job, doing something he has always wanted to do.

(3) One clergyman asked another for the name of a good psychoanalyst. He was involved in a worthwhile

ministry, helping the world's dispossessed, but he felt that his relationships were superficial and that he was often ineffective. His friend suggested that he try "openness" with one other person as a last resort before beginning psychoanalysis. "Tell this person everything God has revealed to you about your own life — even the thing you said you'd never tell anyone." "Even that?" "Even that," was the rejoinder, though the second man had no inkling what "that" was. The experience which followed of depth fellowship and honesty led to a whole new life for the clergyman. He already knew Christ and Christian theology, but he needed the power of confession in order to find release.

If we can relate to people in terms of where they really are, rather than on the basis of their symptoms, we will approach Jesus' own method of dealing with people. For example, most alcoholics have a great need for love. Rather than scolding and shaming them, we need to supply a relationship of love which gets to the heart of their problem. Self-righteous people who are always impressing us with their good works usually need approval. Those easily irritated are really saying, "You don't love me enough." The person taking drugs or involved in illicit sex is trying to escape, saying, "I can't stand the hurt of life the way it is."

In Katherine Anne Porter's *Ship of Fools*, one of the characters, a wealthy, self-sufficient divorcee, expresses herself in a bitter but poignant monologue: "Love me. Love me in spite of all! Whether or not I love you, whether I am fit to love, whether you are able to love, even if there is no such thing as love, love me!" When we can hear the sophisticated, the cynical, the hard, the bitter, or the escapist saying this, and can relate to him on this basis, we will practice the art of conversation in the way our Lord did.

A conversation with a psychiatrist has helped me greatly in recent months. He said, "I am convinced that there is no such thing as mental illness. What we call mental illness is only an attempt to grow. In trying to restore the patient to a former state, the doctor and the family often do more harm than good. If we can identify and live with him through this time of growth, he will emerge a better person, more mature, and more whole." It is this kind of insight which can help us to further Christ's work of wholeness and healing and to be, in effect, His very channel for such growth.

After we have begun to understand another person, and to analyze what he has and what he lacks, *it is important that we know what to do and what to say, and what to be in the relationship.* Certainly we must identify ourselves as fellow discoverers of the love and power of God. This requires some personal honesty about our own needs and struggles.

Also, we must listen. There is no better way to communicate to a person a sense of his own worth and dignity before God than to listen to the nature and the shape of his struggle.

Along with listening, an occasional question can illuminate for someone his hidden motive, desire, need, or guilt. Jesus' miraculous healing of the Gerasene demoniac began with a question (Luke 8:26-39).

Dr. Robert Sterling Palmer, a Boston physician, in

doing a test of four hundred run-of-the-mill patients, discovered that in many cases asking the right questions produced better results than pills and medicine. The three questions he asked most often were: (1) Do you ever ask yourself what you are getting out of life? (2) Do you ever ask yourself the meaning of life? (3) Do you have a sense of dread or foreboding, panic or terror? As people answered these questions, many tended to discover the psychic and emotional roots behind their physical illnesses.

If a doctor finds that such questions can produce healing more effectively than drugs, then we Christians can certainly use the same method in our ministry of healing. One doesn't need a medical license to ask questions. Sometimes in conversation we need to ask the person what it is he wants most out of life, or what he is dreaming and hoping for. To ask a man about his dreams may give us the privilege of interpreting God to him.

One summer I met a radiant woman, and I asked her about the turning point in her life. She said that several years before someone had asked her, "Does the world need another person like you?" She confessed that at the time she was the gloomiest, sourest, most negative person imaginable. When she replied, "No," and admitted that she really didn't want to be that kind of person either, her friend, skilled in the art of conversation, said, "I think your real name is 'Sunshine.'" Almost from that moment on, the woman became her new name. This illustrates the art of conversation at its best.

The keys of the Kingdom are in the hands of believers. God has so decreed it. He says that those whom we let in come in, and those whom we keep out are kept out. This is a terrible responsibility, but it is also the greatest privilege in the world. There is nothing more exciting than practicing the art of conversation, so that through relationships others may discover their true selves and the God who loves them.

3. THE ART OF INTRODUCTION

ONE OF MY PAINFUL MEMORIES is of an introduction which took place many years ago. As I introduced two prominent men to each other at a reception, stage fright and self-consciousness overwhelmed me. I couldn't remember the name of one, and the credentials of the other got twisted. Blushing and stammering, I hurried off, only dimly aware that the two people were happily getting to know each other.

Of course we all want to be socially skillful, able to bring together people of varying backgrounds and traditions in a gracious, comfortable manner and to help them to meet and discover each other. But even an awkward, painful introduction accomplishes its purpose.

In the instance I have mentioned, a relationship began which has been of great use to God and His Kingdom. My part was in one sense crucial and in another unimportant. Without me these two men might never have met; they would have missed a great friendship and God would have missed a usable team. Yet I am sure that both of them have forgotten by now who introduced them. I alone remember the introduction and my embarrassment.

Jesus Christ is a living person; not a theory, nor a law, nor a theological truth. Theology is important for a more complete understanding of Christ, but the Christian life begins when we are introduced to *the* Friend. It is that simple.

Nothing is more needed today in the Church than introducers. When you know Christ as a person, you can introduce Him to another and trust that He will be as eager to reveal Himself as my two friends were in spite of my awkward introduction.

There is freedom if we realize that proper titles and definitive terms about Christ are unnecessary in the art of introduction. A scientist friend of mine tells about one of his colleagues who was intrigued by the Christian life through contact with a lunch-hour group meeting in his lab. After many months he came to my friend and said he wanted to find the kind of life he had seen in this small group of men. "I know that commitment is the answer," he announced, "but I don't believe in God, let alone Jesus Christ, so how can I find what you have found?"

"Tell me, can you make a turnip?" my friend asked, remembering something he had heard elsewhere.

"Of course not."

"Do you know of anyone who can make a turnip?"

"No."

"Well, will you turn your life over to the person who makes turnips?"

The man did exactly that. And then Jesus Christ —

the author and creator of all things, the "turnip maker"
— began to reveal Himself. Through joining the group
and reading the Bible regularly, the man in a short time
acquired much Biblical and doctrinal knowledge, but
this knowledge about Christ came *after* the introduction.

The Church today is like a corporation with a marvelous advertising campaign but very few salesmen in the
field. An ever-increasing number of people have discovered Life and can witness compellingly, humorously,
and effectively about Christ. But where are the introducers?

It is high adventure to stand by while a person meets
the Person and begins a new style of life. Here are three
suggestions which may prove helpful in acquiring the
art of introduction:

First, new life can start when a person begins a relationship with Jesus Christ in which, for him, there are
no conscious reservations. Our job is not to anticipate
the things in someone's life which may need to be dealt
with, but to suggest that he give Christ all he sees at the
moment.

Second, suggest that this commitment to Christ be as
specific as possible.

Third, encourage your friend to make this commitment aloud in your presence — even as marriage vows
are exchanged in the presence of witnesses.

One of the most effective Christians I know is a garage owner on Long Island. Though he was a church
member, Al resisted turning his life over to "new management." Then one night, after a long conversation
with a friend who was a newspaper editor in a nearby

town, the editor said, "Well, Al, if you are satisfied with your life the way it is, forget about this commitment to Christ."

Al was troubled for days. He had many doctrinal questions about the person of Christ and the necessity for commitment, but he was not satisfied with his life. Some days later he returned to his editor friend, and met Jesus Christ as his Lord.

Recently I met a skeptical young man who had just been discharged from the Marine Corps. George seemed so negative about everything Christian that it surprised me when he confided that he was secretly reading many books about Christ, but was not convinced.

"I want to know if Jesus Christ is real," he said. "If He is, I want to give Him my life. If not, I want to forget all about this stuff."

I suggested an experiment: that if there really was someone called Christ who loved George and was eager to give him new life, He could make Himself known in many convincing ways. But if there was no such person, the experiment would make that obvious.

"I'll buy that," he answered. We bowed our heads and after a long pause George said something like this: "Jesus, I don't know if You are real, but if You are and if You can hear me and if You care for me, I turn my life over to You unreservedly."

When George looked up there were tears in his eyes, and he said, "I hope He is real!"

After a bit, I asked, "How will you know if your life has been changed? You can't depend on feelings, because they come and go. What are some things that will be different if Christ has taken charge?"

He thought for a minute and mentioned several obvious things that would be typical of most young men. Then he said, "I will *really* know that I am different if I can love my dad when I drive him home from the factory tomorrow. Every day he lectures me on how I should work harder, apply myself more, and not be a failure. He means well, but his sermons bug me, and I sit there seething with resentment."

Later in the week a letter came telling of a whole new relationship between the young man and his father. Christ revealed Himself to George in a way he could understand.

The Long Island editor was very wise when he stopped arguing doctrine with the garage owner and said, "Are you satisfied with your life the way it is?" This is a much more effective approach than trying to convince a skeptic that Jesus was born of a virgin, walked on water, turned water into wine, and all the rest.

There are many questions that God will give us at the right moment to move the issue from the doctrinal to the volitional. One such question is, "What do you want to do with your life?" Someone has said, "More people are kept from the Kingdom of God by cold feet than by cold logic."

As with George, the Marine, it is helpful to get people to express the specific things in their lives which they know are wrong and which need to be changed. This is how we affirm that Jesus Christ is the Evangelist, and that He has spoken to the person long before we entered the picture. The skillful introducer will give the other person a chance to report those things and to nail them down.

There is no fixed pattern or sequence in the art of introduction. Once a man drove two hundred miles to see me for the express purpose of giving his life to Christ. For two hours we sat in my study while I asked him to tell me the things in his life that needed changing, but he kept insisting, "I can't think of a thing."

I probed and probed until I almost killed the patient. Finally I asked, "Well, why don't we get on with the business of commitment?" "That's what I came for," he replied. As we knelt together, this man made a stumbling but genuine surrender — and *then* for the next half hour he poured out the habits, fears, sins, and wrong relationships of a lifetime.

D. T. Niles says that evangelism is simply one beggar telling another where to find bread.* If in introducing, we realize we are not teaching great doctrinal truths, the issue becomes relatively simple. It is simple because Christ Himself is the Evangelist, and we merely co-operate with Him.

We must seek spiritual skills as earnestly as we seek social skills. But the important thing is to begin now to be introducers. Introducing others to Christ is normal Christianity. The fun begins when we start to practice the art of introduction.

* *That They May Have Life* (New York: Harper & Row, Inc., 1961), p. 96.

4. | THE ART OF CHRISTIAN STRATEGY

THE UNITED STATES ARMY has discovered a new strategy in recent years for treating combat soldiers who have mental or emotional breakdowns. Instead of transporting them to a quiet, well-equipped army hospital far removed from the front line, army doctors now treat them in makeshift tent hospitals only a mile or two from the battle zone. It has been found that the farther a soldier is removed from his unit the longer his treatment will take, and the less likely is his chance of recovery. The reason for this is now clear: instead of being labeled a "mental case" and becoming a statistic in an army hospital, the soldier feels that he is still a member of a fighting unit only a short distance away, and that he will soon return to it. Also, he sees himself as a sick person, not a psychotic, and this helps him to maintain his identity and self-respect.

This insight is responsible for the new strategy in dealing with mental illness, as large state mental hospitals are phased out and smaller community mental health centers are built. So we see that even in the medical realm, it is not enough to desire health for a person or a group of people. We must discover the particular strategy through which God brings healing.

God has goals for persons and groups in every situation. Such goals are recognizable and realizable. He also has a strategy for fulfilling these goals. The combination of right goals, sincerity, and zeal do not always accomplish the desired ends. Too often we Christians either have no sense of strategy or use the wrong strategy. We need to learn constantly from our Lord's example and from the Holy Spirit's leading.

A careful study of the gospels reveals much of the strategy Jesus used in helping people to achieve God's goals for their lives. Let me suggest several aspects of Jesus' strategy in His ministry to individuals, to groups, and to society. These will in no way be exhaustive, but they may indicate that there is an effective strategy to achieve legitimate goals for each person or group for whom we feel responsible, and for whose good we want to work.

Harry Emerson Fosdick has said that every man is like an island; if we are to help him to discover his identity and God's plan for his life, we must "row around him" until we find a suitable place to land. This may take a few minutes or it may take years. Each man has a landing place where we can make contact with him and establish a beachhead for what God ultimately intends.

One obvious strategy in Jesus' life is His emphasis on the cost of discipleship. He seemed to spend more time warning men of perils and difficulties than He did in urging them to follow Him. He warned people to count the cost, and said, "Remember, the foxes have holes but the Son of Man has nowhere to lay his head."

Our Lord wants us to know that following Him will cost far more than we first imagined. But this also indicates that Jesus knows people. We are always suspicious of the hard sell, something-for-nothing offer. When we tell people of the cost and peril of a life of discipleship, we challenge something deep and basic in them.

When the Italian patriot Garibaldi was recruiting his army, he threw out a wonderful challenge which evoked an overwhelming response both in loyalty and in numbers. "Soldiers, what I have to offer you is fatigue, danger, struggle, and death; the chill of the cold night in the free air, and heat under the burning sun; no lodging, no munitions, no provisions, but forced marches, dangerous watch posts, and continual struggle with bayonets against batteries. Those who love freedom and their country may follow me." Few men could resist such a challenge to offer their lives in a great and worthy cause.

This is the kind of thing Jesus kept saying, but it is often missed by Christians today. We tell people how much they will receive and how wonderful the Church is, and how secure the Christian life is. Not only are these partial truths, but such promises set up psychological blocks for many people. Of the churches I have known, those which have made the requirements for church membership difficult and strenuous have had the greatest success in recruiting members.

A businessman in Pittsburgh told how Sam Shoemaker challenged him to love members of his family who had hurt him deeply. He felt his resentment was justifiable, and he was not about to love or forgive. But instead of scolding or sympathizing, Sam dared him to pray for these people at least once a day for thirty days. Responding to the dare, the young man found that prayer not only changed him but also changed his relatives, and a relationship of mutual love and respect was initiated.

Second, we find that Jesus often made contact with people by asking for help. He asked the Samaritan woman by the well if she would give Him a drink of water. He asked the hated and miserable tax collector, Zacchaeus, if he would feed Him and His men. Often we Christians try to help people in need only to find that this drives them away and alienates them further. If we employ Jesus' method and ask someone for help, we can give a needy person dignity and a sense of worth which will enable him, at some future time, to talk about his own problems.

My son Peter, now twelve years old, is a vigorous and active boy scout. He hikes and camps out with other scouts in all kinds of weather. Occasionally they have a father-and-son campout, and I am always reluctant to go because I am embarrassed by my ineptness in the woods and lack of camping skills. On one of these excursions I was amazed to find that my son was prepared for every emergency and even equipped to provide luxuries for me. I was impressed by his skills and kept telling him so. The climax came on Saturday night as we finished a roast chicken dinner which we ate with our fingers. The washhouse was hundreds of yards away and our hands were a sticky mess, but Peter produced a pre-moistened "towelette" from his pocket and said, "Here, Dad." He had not forgotten a thing.

My unashamed praise of his foresight and skill provided the basis for a wonderful conversation as we turned in for the night in our pup tent. It was one of the best times Peter and I had ever had together.

The Bible tells us it is more blessed to give than to receive. It is also more fun, and *we need to love other people enough to let them have this kind of fun*. We often build a relationship best when we are on the receiving end of someone's love and concern.

Third, we find that honesty is an important part of the strategy Jesus used with individuals. I am thinking here especially of His relationship with the twelve disciples. In trying to make them the kind of men who would establish the Kingdom following His ascension, He talked about His own past and present needs and fears. We know of Jesus' temptation in the wilderness because He told His disciples about it. In the Garden of Gethsemane He told Peter and James and John that He was troubled, fearful, and anxious, and that He needed their prayers and support.

Too many Christian leaders today are reluctant to share their needs and struggles with those whom they are training and teaching. This is a mistake. We must learn that honesty about our own difficulties can be a source of help and learning for others.

An effective preacher is supposed to "comfort the afflicted and afflict the comfortable." Jesus certainly employed this strategy in relation to the groups of people with whom He lived. He often scolded and rebuked the "good people" of His time, those who made up the religious "establishment." Jesus called many spiritual leaders "whitewashed tombs . . . full of dead men's bones" (Matthew 23:27). He understood that to encourage people in false or shallow piety was to fail them. He loved and understood people enough to practice the strategy of scolding the best people. If in our churches we praise those who are law-abiding and scold the drunkards and adulterers, our strategy is all wrong.

At best, our goals for people are the same as Jesus' goals. When a group of townspeople were about to stone a woman taken in adultery, Jesus' own gentleness with her was an affront to the "good people." It still is. His acceptance of people like Mary Magdalene and Zacchaeus certainly must have been shocking. But the only way to measure strategy is in results, and with these people He brought about a commitment of their lives to Him as Lord, and to their neighbor as brothers and servants.

During a three-day church conference, a gifted Christian woman stayed at the home of a friend of mine who was resisting the challenge of total discipleship. One night he turned to his guest and said, "Alicia, I'm a good man. I really am! Ask anybody, even the members of my family, and they will tell you. I tithe my income, I serve in church, I'm good to people, I'm honest." Instead of pointing out that the Bible says, "All have sinned," and that certainly the man must have all kinds of unrecognized sins, this wise and winsome woman said, "Ben, I know you are good. I have seen over these three days just how really good you are. As a matter of fact, you're one of the best men I've ever met. I've been deeply impressed by the quality of your life. Why don't you commit your life to Jesus Christ?" Ben said, "Yes, let's do it right now." And he did.

Max, a prospector in the Hudson Bay area of northern Canada, began the Christian life some years ago. He has influenced many people, both the sophisticated suburbanites of Toronto, where he and his family live, and the rough and ready men who prospect with him in the bush country. I once asked Max what his strategy was in helping some of his rugged co-workers to find Christ. He thought for a minute and then said, "Well, when a man comes to work in the morning bragging of some exploit or indulgence of the night before, I just tell him, 'Don't stand on the hose!'" Instead of shaming a man for his sins, Max implies that God loves him, and that every time he sins against a neighbor by dishonesty or immorality, he is "standing on the hose," preventing the God who loves him from blessing him.

Jesus often did the unexpected. Remember that when the disciples of John the Baptist asked Jesus for His credentials, He did not mention such things as knowledge of the law or zealousness in prayer. Rather, He emphasized that the sick were healed, the lepers cleansed, the blind made to see, and that the poor had good news preached to them (Luke 7:18-23). He did not discount piety, but emphasized a needed ministry to one who might over-focus on the spiritual aspects of life. On the other hand, we find that Jesus discussed spiritual things with the most carnal and earthy people. He brought the missing ingredient to the individuals with whom He came in contact.

It takes a great deal of freedom and love to be shockingly therapeutic with a group. Many years ago when Emil Brunner, the great Swiss theologian, was lecturing in this country, it was reported that when he preached in so-called "liberal" seminaries he enjoyed dropping "proof texts" from the Bible, and at more conservative or "fundamentalist" schools he smoked big black cigars. He loved people enough to want to jar them out of their stereotyped thinking. He wanted them to be aware that life in Christ was broader than the particular thing they had discovered.

Finally, let us examine Jesus' strategy with corporate groups of people, such as His nation and, by implication, the world at large. A number of things become obvious. First, we see that He began His ministry at the "grass roots" rather than at the "top." He lived with and worked with and taught the little people. He called them to purity and repentance and reform. Often today we want to begin reform at the top without providing clinical examples of what we are aiming for. It is important that we establish a base with ordinary people before we confront power structures.

Second, Jesus set out to change the world by building a small team. This group of twelve became the primary focus of His ministry. He lavished most of His time on them. The mass media of communication are important — and it is certainly imperative that Christians make use of them whenever possible — but history demonstrates that a team of people obedient to Christ and committed to one another in love and fellowship is much more effective than a lone crusader, however highly publicized.

Third, Jesus aimed at the very center of the power structures of His time. He went right to Jerusalem and into the temple where authority lay. Most of His time was not spent there, but it is obvious that all through His ministry His eyes were on the target. We cannot work only at the grass roots. We must keep in mind the centers of authority from which come most of the forces that shape society. Many of us who are person-centered are content to stay only at the grass roots, forgetting that people are often victims of systems or structures which must ultimately be challenged and attacked.

A fourth strategy our Lord employed was to challenge publicly the popular lies, myths, and half-truths of His time. He did not write tracts or books but stood up before the religious establishment in the presence of the people and said the things that were true. Of course this is what led to His betrayal and death. But if we are to have a God-guided ministry that will make lasting changes in the world, we must risk our lives and reputations and all the rest and maintain our convictions in public as well as in private.

A fifth and final strategy was Jesus' self-sacrifice. When it was obvious that if He continued His teaching He would be destroyed, He did not retreat to some safe place. He sacrificed Himself, and by this sacrifice men found new life and the Kingdom was established.

In the garden when the soldiers came for Jesus, He said to them, "I am he — the man you are seeking." Then He pointed to the twelve and said, "Let these men go"

(John 18:5-8). This kind of strategy is something that all serious reformers must understand. It is *our lives* and *our fortunes* we must offer, not other people's. This is true for nations which would be obedient to God, as well as for individuals.

Christians, obedient to their Lord and guided by the Holy Spirit, are attacking and challenging some of the power structures of our time. An executive in a large corporation had his life changed by Alcoholics Anonymous, and then became aware that his company had no rehabilitation program for alcoholics. As he saw colleagues fired because they could not get the help they needed and in many cases wanted, he devised a strategy to plant an idea in the minds of the medical authorities of his company. Today that company has a large and flourishing program for the rehabilitation of alcoholics. Very few people know that this man was responsible for a program which has been of help to countless others. For years I have kept a card on my desk which says, "There is no limit to the amount of good a man can do if he doesn't care who gets the credit."

A gifted minister found much division in his church between the official board and the people who were finding the Christian life for the first time. Many of the people to whom he had ministered and to whom Christ had brought liberty and freedom were non-church members or marginal church members. They eventually formed a large and powerful group, but the establishment at the center of the corporate organization of the church remained largely untouched by his ministry.

This produced a problem which was never really resolved.

On being called to a new church, the minister decided to copy the Apostle Paul. As Paul went from city to city, he always approached the Jewish leaders first to preach and teach. Only when he was rejected by them did he turn to the Gentiles. So this man spent the first year of his ministry in the new church working only with the official board. He resisted requests for counseling and help from people who were on the fringes of the church. Now, several years later, the new life in that church and in that town centers in the official board. The people on the fringes have been blessed, often by the lay witness from members of the official board. The strategy has proved sound, and the church has an authentic lay ministry without divisive factions.

Too often we try to build a new relationship with someone and fail because we go at it the wrong way. In my early struggling years as a Christian, many people had answers for my life and were eager to point out things I should do or stop doing. But when I met a group of people who were sensitive to God's strategy, they accepted me wholeheartedly and loved me enthusiastically. This was Jesus own method and it *still* is His method with His people. Because I was accepted, I was secure enough ultimately to confess my sins and to claim power and release in the Holy Spirit.

As we pray for authentic and right goals in seeking to help individuals or groups, it's important to know that the Holy Spirit is a strategist. We must learn His unique ways of achieving His goals in and through us.

5. THE ART OF COMMUNICATION

IN THE DAYS WHEN Yogi Berra was the manager of a baseball team, one of the players was quoted as saying, "Yogi knows more about baseball than all of the team put together. It's too bad he doesn't know how to tell us about it." It is also too bad when committed and knowledgeable Christians don't know how to communicate the central meaning of their own life in Christ in understandable ways to their neighbors, friends, and colleagues.

In Jesus' last appearance to His followers, as reported in the Book of Acts, He said simply, "You shall be my witnesses . . ." (Acts 1:8).

The word "witness" has always scared some Christians. They think of people in unnatural circumstances making peculiar statements and applying pressure on others. But to witness means simply to communicate.

It is true that communication can be illusory. A teacher on the first day of school, explaining the rules and regulations of school life to her kindergarten class, said, "Now, if any of you have to go to the bathroom, raise your hand." A startled youngster in the back row asked, "How will that help?" We make assumptions about what others will understand, and feel certain we're doing an excellent job of communicating, only to find out that we have been thoroughly misunderstood.

The Church faces the danger of irrelevancy and non-communication in every age — certainly in our own. The Sunday school, for example, is now undergoing severe criticism and reappraisal. Educators and church leaders in every denomination are discovering that their expensive curricula are often irrelevant and do not speak to youngsters or adults in a language they can understand.

Preaching has come under the same kind of attack. It has often been said that preachers are answering questions nobody is asking. At any rate they too rarely talk about things which have meaning for the man in the pew.

But now let us consider witnessing, not as teachers or preachers, but from the point of view of the layman who is on the frontier of the Church in his daily life.

Recently I have contacted about twenty of the most gifted "communicators" I know, both lay people and clergy. They are men and women who are capable of communicating the truth of the Christian life in natural and relevant ways. Their "secrets" will be found in the following pages.

First of all, what are we charged by our Lord to communicate? Simply the reality and power and love of God as we know it in Jesus Christ, our contemporary. This astounding fact is communicated best relationally, not propositionally. People observe in us the results of our relationship to Christ, and are either intrigued or repelled. Teaching is secondary and usually follows only as people are impelled to ask questions. The old saying, "What you are speaks so loudly that I can't hear what you say," is still true.

Some years ago I was a part of a businessmen's luncheon group in which much of the conversation among the newer men dealt with ideas and theories about God and Christian ethics. One of the men who talked about a relationship to Christ requiring his total commitment often seemed to go unheard. But one day this man left his job, which in those days paid him the magnificent sum of $13,000 a year, to work for a Christian mission paying only a small fraction of that amount. We all knew he had a retarded child who required expensive care. Immediately everything that he had been saying for months as a prosperous businessman took on new meaning. What he *did* communicated far better than all he had previously *said* about the reality and trustworthiness of God.

It has been said that no one is ever argued into the Kingdom of God. Arguments are almost never helpful, but simple answers to life's basic questions, given at the right time, can be a key in the hands of a seeker.

The turning point in the life of Gert Behanna, the author of *The Late Liz,* began when she was invited by a wealthy friend in Connecticut to come and meet some people from her own social set who had had a vital experience of God. She had never met such people before, and got thoroughly drunk in preparation for the ordeal. As the dinner party progressed, Gert found herself chattering about all of the unfair and unjust things that had been happening to her. Tom and Blanche Page listened quietly. Finally Tom said, "Gert, you certainly have a lot of problems. Why don't you turn them all over to God?" Gert was shocked, and asked, "Do you mean like turning my luggage over to a redcap?" "Exactly!" Tom replied. Some days later, back in her Illinois home, Gert Behanna got on her knees and did just that. It was the beginning of a remarkable conversion.

When are we to be His witnesses or to communicate? Remember that Jesus concluded His final words with the injunction to begin in Jerusalem, the place where the early disciples lived. To us, this means that we are to begin where *we* live, with friends and family and colleagues. This is certainly the most difficult place to witness, but also the most rewarding. The people who know us best are either the most intrigued by our style of life or the most suspicious that what we are does not measure up to what we say. If Jesus Christ has made a difference in us, the people with whom we live and work will know it.

While serving in my first church after my ordination, I met a surgeon who had a great influence on my life. He was the senior vestryman in a local Episcopal church and also part of an ecumenical men's group which met weekly. Most of all, he was a communicator of the love, power, and healing of God in his everyday life. Nurses and interns who worked with him said that he was a perfectionist and "hard as nails," but he prayed before and during every operation and he was able to communicate both verbally and non-verbally the love and power of God to his patients.

One day I asked the doctor when he had become aware of the reality of Jesus Christ. After a long pause, he said, "When I was a boy. My father never made more than forty dollars a week in his whole life, but every Sunday morning in church I saw him put a ten-dollar bill in the collection plate!" This is the kind of communication that profoundly affects our children and all those around us.

Another opportunity for effective communication comes when the person we are with, stranger or friend, expresses a real need or concern. Our response to needs communicates a great deal. If Jesus Christ has begun to meet our own needs, then we communicate verbally or non-verbally to others that we know that He is concerned about particular problems, and that He has answers for them. *We* don't have the answer, but we can communicate our confidence that God has direction and guidance and is eager to give it.

A government lawyer in Washington, D.C., illustrates how this can take place. Years ago, as a partner in private practice, he began to drink heavily. Before long he became a confirmed alcoholic, and as a result lost his practice and finally his wife. Through an experience of Christ and membership in Alcoholics Anonymous, he began a new life. He was reunited with his wife and rehired by his old firm as a very lowly staff member. As such, he was given a "hopeless" case in which his firm represented one of two large corporations which had been deadlocked in legal proceedings for several years.

One day the lawyer called together the legal advisers for both parties and simply related the story of how God had solved the insoluble problem of his own life. He suggested that most of the men in the room also believed in God, and affirmed his conviction that there was a solution for the very involved problem which was costing both corporations a great deal of time and money. He called for some minutes of quiet in which each man would ask God in his own way what he could do to help solve the problem.

Half an hour later the case was resolved to the satisfaction of both parties. Partly as a result of this incident, a fruitful career in government began for the attorney. God continues to help both individuals and corporations through the guided counsel of this contemporary communicator.

Christians can also find opportunities for witness when someone expresses criticism. Instead of scolding the person for his negative attitude, or sympathizing with him for the apparent injustice, we may be able to ask what he feels he can do to help solve the particular situation or to help the one who is offending him. Because Jesus Christ has helped us with our resentments, jealousies, and criticisms, we can communicate that He has an answer for others.

Two of the most effective communicators I know are men who have inner-city ministries. Bill Milliken works on the Lower East Side of New York City. Bill Iverson ministers to young people in the heart of Newark. Both have identified with minority groups who have much justifiable resentment against society, and particularly

against white people. These two white men have identified effectively with non-whites and are challenging
them to be part of the answer instead of part of the problem. Our opportunities may not be as dramatic, but they
are just as relevant.

Finally, the normal conversations of everyday life are
far better opportunities for communication than are con-
trived situations. The Church has often tried to create
times of witness during religious services or other somewhat artificial occasions. My wife and I know a remarkable couple whose lives were changed dramatically during Billy Graham's first crusade in New York. This well-
to-do, well-educated, and attractive couple were intrigued by a friend, a fashion model, newly married,
who told them in normal conversation about the change
that had taken place in her life and in her marriage because of Jesus Christ. This prompted them to go to a
Billy Graham meeting, where they themselves began a
relationship with Christ.

Returning home full of enthusiasm, they tried inviting
their friends in to a weekly Bible study group, but the
results were a dismal failure. After many such artificial
attempts, they began to learn that it is in the everyday
relationships of life that people communicate most effectively, just as their friend had done. These two have
since become the center of a whole group of couples who
are discovering the reality and power of Jesus Christ.

Certainly there is a time for "visitation campaigns"
and for special services in the church. But twentieth-
century Christians are discovering, as did their first-
century counterparts, that the most effective and rele-

vant communication or witnessing can take place in the market place, at the country club, in the union hall, in the supermarket, and in the office.

Let us consider the actual ways and means of communicating to others. We affirm again that some non-verbal communication must first take place. It is what we do and are, not what we say, that has an impact on people.

Thousands of Americans and even people from other countries know of Ralston Young, recently retired Red Cap 42 at Grand Central Station. This man has discovered authentic communication on the job and has been an example to many of discipleship in our day. His conversations with passengers and his thrice-weekly meetings in an unlighted railroad coach have inspired many of us to put our faith to work.

A Canadian woman confided that several years ago she decided to leave her husband and children and run off with a man who was also leaving his family. They left home and were about to begin a new life under different names. Walking through the great concourse of Grand Central Station, where they were to change trains, they happened to look up and see Red Cap 42. They had both heard him speak at a conference some time previously. Just the sight of him was a witness to the Lord whom he served. Turning to her companion, the woman said, "We cannot go through with this. We must return to our families."

Non-verbal communication can be powerful. A layman I know got a call at midnight. A friend of his was drunk and threatening his wife with a gun. The layman rushed over with great fear but with much faith to confront his friend and fellow church member. For two hours he witnessed about his own Christian experience and then he recounted every Bible story that he could recall. He shamed and threatened the man, but all to no avail. Finally, utterly defeated, and frightened that the man might succeed in his attempt to murder his wife and possibly others, he put his arms around his friend's neck and wept. The second man recounted later that it was this loving demonstration which finally got to him. It was not the words but the tears and the concern which convinced him that God cared for him.

But witness at some point must also be verbal. Here are some ingredients I consider important for verbal communication.

(1) *Be intriguing, intelligent, and relevant when you speak about Jesus Christ.* A pious tone or artificial words do not communicate the reality of Christian faith.

(2) *Use the language of the other person.* We must remember that the original Greek of the New Testament was the language of the street, not the language of scholars. Elizabethan English, the language of the King James Bible, is not the language that Americans use today. The truths of the Bible are much greater than any attempt, past or present, to describe them. We must learn to use the language of our day to speak about eternal truths, even as Jesus and the first-century apostles did.

(3) *Be enthusiastic and sincere when you witness.* This certainly cannot be artificially generated. When we are genuinely enthusiastic about who Christ is, what He

has done for us, and what He can do for another, effective communication takes place.

(4) *Try to start with a point of agreement.* Even someone hostile to God or the Church will say something with which we can agree. When Harry Emerson Fosdick got into conversation with a man who professed to be an atheist, Fosdick said, "Tell me about the god you don't believe in. Perhaps I don't believe in him either." That was a starting point for relevant communication.

(5) *Express a part of your own needs or of God's answer which somehow touches on the other person's condition.* "Total recall" is unnecessary and will only bore him. Tell that part of your experience that most nearly matches the place where he is struggling right now.

(6) *Ask questions.* This helps the person to talk through his own doubts and fears, as well as his hopes and aspirations. Remember that Jesus was a master in the use of questions.

(7) *Help him to clarify his needs,* to get behind his hurt or jealousy or resentment and tell you what this has triggered in him to make him bitter or depressed at the moment. This enables the person to understand himself and to find a beginning point in his own life where God's answers may apply.

(8) *Don't assume anything.* The person is neither as good nor as bad as he appears to be. Find out what he really believes and feels, and what he wants for his life. One of the best questions might be, "What do you most want to get out of life?" This can disarm even a militant

atheist, who may begin to share his aspirations with you. In the same way, don't assume that because someone is a church member he believes all the things his church teaches. By assuming nothing, we let the person speak for himself and clarify his own position in our presence.

(9) *Don't criticize the person for what he is doing or saying.* Try to guide him into some kind of helpful approach that will help him be the person he has told you he wants to be.

(10) *Help him to make a decision.* After he has talked through his problems, hopes, and fears, help him to find a beginning point where he can trust God. It may be an initial decision to turn his life over to Christ, or it may be some next step that will let God take him deeper into the Christian life. Try to pray *with* him, rather than *for* him. Ten words of prayer from him in your hearing will mean more to him than an hour's sermonizing or teaching from you.

(11) *Follow up on this friend frequently in the days that follow.* Have lunch with him, call him, write to him, put him in touch with others if he doesn't live near you. Let him know that God cares and that you care. Encourage him to write to you or to call you often. Let him know that there will be discouragements and setbacks, but that these are normal and he should not fear them.

Finally, let us consider the underlying preparation for communication or witnessing. Since none of us knows at what moment God will give us an opportunity to be His witness, we must always be prepared and on the alert.

First, check your own motives and attitudes. Remember that you are "one beggar telling another beggar where to find bread." This does not glorify you as a witness, but establishes you as one who is witnessing about life and health to another who is also struggling.

Second, think through or write out your own experience. When you have put down everything that God has demonstrated in His relationship with you, you will have at your fingertips a number of vignettes or experiences that can be brought forward at the right time to help someone else. Too many of us tell our entire story and simply swamp someone with experiences and ideas that are not relevant to him.

Third, develop a friendship with the person — or begin with someone whose friendship you have already won. A visitation campaign is difficult because it often involves conversations which are artificial. But even in this situation a few words can begin a friendship.

Learn to cooperate with the Holy Spirit. Believe that God has been working on each person from the very day of his birth. God can use us to say the "next thing" that someone is ready to hear about himself or God. It is arrogant to assume that we are the first contact he has had with God, and such an assumption can make us superficial and unloving. Let us believe that we are one of God's many agents who will speak and relate to the person's past, present, and future.

Finally, believe in the other person's potential greatness through God. Perhaps this is the most important thing of all. If we believe someone is hopeless, we communicate this. But if, having heard the worst, we believe that God has a plan and an answer for him, even as for us, this too comes across. The person can then take heart and find hope, and be open to hearing whatever we have to say.

Any willing Christian has adequate credentials to be a witness. We need to overcome our self-consciousness and insecurity. To let a sense of inadequacy keep us from being ministers to others is a sin. If someone begins to speak of his needs, believe that God can communicate through you some vital thing to help him at that moment.

A bailiff in a Canadian city has discovered God's plan for his life, and he and his wife have had a group meeting in their home for years. One day, with great trepidation, he invited an atomic scientist working on a government project to join the group. The day after the meeting the bailiff sought out the scientist and asked about his reactions. The scientist, who was a bit of an agnostic, had been thrilled by the evening and had found real help, especially in something that had been said by another member of the group, an illiterate Indian.

This is the miracle of God's communicating through His people. The young can speak to the old, and the uneducated to the educated. God wants His people to be witnesses. He calls us to be the individuals through whom He can speak to contemporary man in his deepest needs.

PART II

6. THE GIFT OF HUMILITY

AT FIVE O'CLOCK on a winter Wednesday I entered New York's Port Authority bus terminal. I was hurrying home for a quick dinner and then on to conduct a midweek service at a nearby church. The usual crowd was lined up behind the escalators that take suburban passengers to their buses. Briefcase in one hand and newspaper in the other, I got in line and began the commuter shuffle.

Just as I got to the head of the line, a hard-faced, middle-aged woman came up from the side, shoved in front of me, planted her elbow in my stomach, and stepped onto the escalator.

Now I maintain that there is nothing easy about the Christian life, and every year I see more clearly the complications of radical obedience to Christ. What should I say to such a person? I know what I would have said a few years ago — but I am no longer free to put someone like that "in his place." I know what I would *like* to say. I would like to be a St. Francis kind of Christian who genuinely loves birds and flowers and little children with sticky lollipops and even pushy middle-aged women — but I haven't arrived at that stage yet.

Being somewhere in between my former condition and my ideal one, I removed the woman's elbow from my stomach and said with elaborate sarcasm, "Forgive me. I didn't mean to shove you."

Her reaction was devastating. She turned, and since she was only a step or two ahead, she looked me straight in the eye. Her face seemed to fall apart — all her wrinkles changed position. "I don't understand it," she said with apology and shock. "Why are you so nice to me? I was really rude — I shouldn't have shoved in line like that."

I was at a loss for words. The woman had reacted to my counterfeit display of love as if it were real, and for the moment, at least, she was transformed. I began to envision this woman as a person who had been fighting all her life for a place in line. Perhaps she had come from a large family where she had been forced to fight for food and favors and affection. Possibly she had been mediocre in studies or social graces and had to fight her way in school. Even now in some office she might be fighting for promotions or benefits or a preferred place on the vacation list. Perhaps this was the first time that someone with whom she was fighting for a place in line had stepped back and given it to her.

At this point I was humiliated by the pettiness of my first reaction and overwhelmed by the effect it had produced, but I gathered my wits enough to mumble something like, "It doesn't hurt to be nice to people." Then I ran headlong for my bus.

As the bus headed for New Jersey, I sat in bewilderment and embarrassment. I had seen myself and the shabbiness of my conduct very clearly. "Lord," I prayed silently, "how can I preach tonight? What are You trying to teach me?"

Finally He seemed to say, "Bruce, I have been trying to tell you, and all My people for centuries, that life upon this earth will not be changed by preaching and teaching and committees, but by people giving up their rightful place in line — every kind of line — simply because I gave up My rightful place when I came to earth to be among you. What I ask is that you who profess to believe in Me do the same. My strategy of love will always release a chain reaction of changed lives."

I never step on the escalator now without looking about wistfully for someone to slam in ahead of me — but no one does! How radically different is what Jesus has in mind for me: He wants me to give up my rightful place in my home, office, professional circle, church, neighborhood. If I am not alert to those who are fighting for first place, my instinct will be to hang on to what is mine, and put the offender in his place. But if I can remember my Lord's strategy and with His help give up what is rightfully mine, I may see miracles.

A leader in the early Church said, "For he is made more worthy who dispenses with what he deserves." More recently, the psychoanalyst William Steckel has said, "The mark of the immature man is that he wants to die nobly for a cause, while the mark of the mature man is that he wants to live humbly for one." It seems that some people in every age have grasped the basic strategy of the incarnation.

The power behind Jesus' revolutionary servanthood is that he chose to become weak and vulnerable. The second chapter of Philippians tells us, "Though he was in the form of God, [he] did not count equality with God a thing to be grasped, but emptied himself, taking the form of a servant, being born in the likeness of men" (2: 6, 7). Jesus the man did not decide to become the Son of God, but the Son of God decided to become Jesus the man. There is a great difference.

A friend of mine who is in his forties said he had been hearing all his life that Christians should deny themselves, turn the other cheek, and lose their lives for others. But only in the last few years, through depth fellowship with Christians in small groups, has he come to have a true sense of his own worth. For the first time he has a life to lose.

This truth is important. If we are submissive because we are frightened and unsure of ourselves, there is nothing dynamic or redemptive in our submission. But when we have the strength and the ability to fight back and then for Christ's sake choose not to do so, power is released in the lives of others. A "Milquetoast" husband is not helping his wife to find emotional maturity, but a man who knows how to give and take in. the rough-and-tumble of marriage, and who then voluntarily submits to his wife, releases God's power in that family.

A father was concerned that his children did not seem to befriend the unlovely ones in school, but sought out only the leaders. As we talked, we decided that there is no virtue in loving the unlovely if they are the only ones who want us. Before children can exercise real Christian virtue and befriend the friendless, they must first be accepted themselves. Only the socially strong can be dynamic servants of the disinherited. There is no virtue in submission if we are too weak to fight. There is no virtue in morality if we are pure only because we fear being caught.

A recent cartoon shows an imposing-looking tycoon leaving church saying to his wife, "Well, all I've got to say is that if the meek are going to inherit the earth, they'd better become a lot more aggressive." In one sense I couldn't agree more. Meekness motivated by fear is not a virtue, but voluntary meekness is the very stuff out of which God will transform His world through His people.

President Johnson has said, "As President [of the United States] you can't go any higher, so you only want to do what's right." I think this parallels precisely the Christian dynamic. Jesus Christ elevates us to the highest position in all creation. From this position of power, we are free to seek to do what is right, rather than to serve our own interests.

A strong-willed and stubborn executive I know fought often and bitterly with his wife about extravagance and mismanagement of funds. When he found faith in Christ, he put his personal funds under her signature in a checking account. To date the wife has not violated this trust, and seeds for a new relationship are being sown.

A New York businessman in his early thirties, in competition for a pending promotion, decided to honor his rival's frequent requests for help and information, simply because he felt this was what God wanted him to do. It is not important to report who got the promotion. What is important is that a man in the middle of the cut-throat competition of today's business world dared to take Jesus Christ seriously when He said, "This is my commandment, that you love one another as I have loved you" (John 15:12).

At a luncheon some time ago a prominent church leader was being discussed by several of the ministers in his denomination. One insisted that though the man was brilliant and dedicated, he was also pompous and stuffy. The argument was settled when another man related that the church leader had once been a guest in his home, and that he had been discovered on his knees playing with the youngest child. Power on its knees is always convincing and compelling. This is the drama of the incarnation.

If the Church is radically to challenge materialism, there must be a large measure of dynamic servanthood in inter-personal relationships. Some years ago in Korea a Y.M.C.A. secretary was killed by a communist youth group. Soon after the violence the killers were caught and brought to trial. However, the dead man's father, a Korean pastor, appeared before the court and pleaded for permission to adopt the leader of the rebel band. His request was granted. This is the kind of dynamic servanthood to which Christ calls all of His people.

God's strategy was to come among us in a costly way in His Son, Jesus Christ. As Christians, we must respond not just with words and ideas but with sacrificial acts that spring from a new heart and a new spirit.

7. | THE GIFT OF FREEDOM

A FEW YEARS AGO I was asked to lead the senior class retreat at Princeton Seminary. This is an annual event and an outstanding Christian minister is usually invited to conduct it.

I did not doubt that I was a person of outstanding ability — but as yet there was little evidence that anyone else had realized it! I had served as pastor of a small church and as assistant pastor of a larger one. I had published no books, nor were my sermons ever quoted. But now, at last, I was sure that my talents had been recognized.

As the retreat began and we were all assembled, I turned confidently to a class officer and asked, "How did you happen to ask me to lead your retreat?"

"Well," he said candidly, "we realized that most of us would never be famous ministers. So this year we decided to ask somebody who had been out of seminary ten years and hadn't made it!"

When Christians are as honest with each other as that young man was with me, a climate is created which makes posturing impossible. Perhaps much of what ordinarily passes for humility and good manners in the church is really a kind of dishonesty which prevents us from knowing God and each other deeply. Freedom to be honest, on the other hand, is one of the most important gifts God gives to His people.

Jesus said, "If the Son makes you free, you will be free indeed" (John 8:36). He Himself certainly lived as a free man.

Have you ever wondered why John the Baptist sent his disciples to ask Jesus if He were the Messiah? John was related to Jesus and knew the extraordinary circumstances of His birth. He baptized Jesus and was present when the Holy Spirit descended, and he heard the voice of God say, "This is my beloved Son." He knew that Jesus had healed the sick and raised the dead and taught with authority.

In spite of all this, while John was in prison, he sent his disciples to question Jesus' authority. (See Luke 7:18-35.) Something must have disturbed him greatly. Perhaps it was the fact that Jesus simply did not conform to the image of Messiah projected by the religious community. Jesus was free to be Himself.

John was a great man, and Jesus Himself said of him, "Among those born of women none is greater than John." As a boy he was separated from his playmates by the Nazarite vow which prevented him from cutting his hair. He was "peculiar" as an adult. He lived much of his life alone in the wilderness, sleeping on the ground, wearing animal skins, and eating grasshoppers. He gloomily renounced the world as he pronounced doom on his generation and called for repentance.

Jesus provided a marked contrast. He went to parties, the Bible indicates that He ate well, wore an expensive garment, and mingled with all kinds of people, including tax collectors, fishermen, prostitutes, and drunkards. In short, while John was the epitome of the so-called religious man, Jesus was not "religious." Perhaps His style of life prompted Dietrich Bonhoeffer, the great German theologian and martyr, to plead for a "religionless Christianity."

Sometimes the freedom which is characteristic of Jesus' disciples is elusive even to the most dedicated Christians. One day I saw an arresting sight on 42nd Street in New York City. A dirty man with long matted hair and a flowing beard was carrying a sandwich board advertising cheap haircuts. The incongruity of this unbarbered man advertising a local barber shop drew many eyes. I smiled at the whimsy of the advertising firm which had hired him, but I was also struck by the tragic similarity to so many of us who proclaim Christian freedom while we remain slaves to the opinions of men.

One barrier to Christian freedom is fear — especially fear of rejection. If we need the approval of men, we are not experiencing the power of God's love and acceptance, which enables us to be free to be what we are and to enjoy life as it comes.

Dr. Howard Keely, who often leads retreats for New England clergymen, uses these four questions as a test of freedom:

(1) *Are you overly concerned about what others think of you?*

(2) *Are you willing to become involved in the world's problems?*

(3) *Are you primarily interested in others for what they can do for you?*

(4) *Are you concerned about who is going to get the credit?*

Our answers to these questions can cut across all our stereotyped ideas of religious do's and don'ts and reveal how fully we have received the gift of freedom.

A second barrier to Christian freedom might be called pseudo-guilt. A genuine sense of guilt which prompts repentance is the beginning of finding God, but there are a number of Christians carrying a great deal of false guilt. For example, I am not a perfect husband, father, son, minister, or friend. Often I feel guilty, but I realize this is neurotic guilt which is destructive, and springs from a false aspiration to perfection.

As I'm caught in this kind of free-floating guilt, I find it helpful to look at the Apostle Paul to see what he was like. Certainly he had all the gifts and fruits of the Holy Spirit. He had a widespread and effective ministry. He is the author of much of the New Testament. But let's do a psychological profile of him from the Biblical record. Let us see what he was not.

(1) *Paul was not perfect.* He had all kinds of arguments and disagreements with fellow Christians and fellow ministers, and he was not an easy person to get along with. He spoke often of his imperfections.

(2) *Paul was not always right.* He had strong convictions, but he was known to compromise in the face of pressure or argument. He said frankly that some of his

opinions were questionable — at least not based on any of Christ's specific commands or teaching (I Corinthians 7; II Corinthians 11).

(3) *Paul's motives were not always pure.* Beginning at Acts 16:16, we find a record of his healing of a demented girl. Luke records that Paul did not heal her when he first saw her, but that she followed him *for many days,* crying out in his meetings. Finally, *out of annoyance,* he healed her. The fact that Paul's true motives are recorded indicates the freedom that characterized life among the first-century Christians. How wonderful it would be if we today could be as free — free to say, "You know I get irritated when Mary calls. She talks and talks endlessly and compulsively. The other day when she called, I was so annoyed that I asked her to come over. When she did, we prayed together and she's beginning to find help!"

(4) *Paul was not impressive as a person.* His preaching was sometimes dull and ineffective. At one point he preached so long that a boy fell off the windowsill and was killed. The lad was restored to life, but Paul was free to let the entire episode be recorded in what has become the Book of Acts (20:7-12). Paul could even accept his own infirmities and claim that Christ's perfection was made perfect in them (II Corinthians 12: 9, 10). He found himself unwelcomed by Jewish leaders as he traveled from synagogue to synagogue, and he often couldn't find acceptance for his ideas among his Christian peers in Jerusalem.

What Paul was not became the occasion of freedom

for God's Spirit! Let us examine the characteristics of this freedom in his life.

(1) *Paul had love.* To love people doesn't necessarily mean to agree with them. Paul gave his life unstintingly for men everywhere. He endured shipwreck, torture, beatings, and imprisonment to carry the message of God's love, even to those who would not accept it. (See II Corinthians 5 and 11.) It has been said that the Cross represents "loving those who don't want you to love them." This is what it meant for Jesus, and this is what it means for those who follow Him.

Paul offered to give up his own eternal salvation if he could win his Jewish brethren to God's love in Jesus Christ (Romans 9). Loving people means giving them what they need, not what they want, even if they turn on you and despise you. For young people today this may mean learning that real love does not mean giving in to sexual demands. To give in may be the very opposite of love. To love is to want God's best for the other person. This may involve keeping one's own standard's at the risk of being misunderstood.

(2) *Paul had great joy.* In prison or on board a sinking ship, he had the joy which comes not from pleasant circumstances but from fellowship with the indwelling Christ who is in control of all situations. (See Philippians 1, Acts 27.)

(3) *Paul had peace.* In the midst of a shipwreck, when even soldiers and sailors were panicky, Paul was at peace. He said grace calmly and began to eat. His quiet confidence, when those who were stronger and

braver were terrified, indicates the dimension of freedom in his life (Acts 27:33-37).

(4) *Paul had authority.* He challenged the ecclesiastical and temporal leaders of his time. Even more impressive, in the shipwreck incident, is the fact that he was obeyed by busy, virile men, in peril of losing their lives. He told the soldiers and sailors what to do and they did it.

(5) *Paul had power* — power to cast out demons, to heal the sick, and to transform lives. His message changed entire churches in a matter of days.

(6) *Finally, Paul was honest, open, and transparent.* He did not have to pretend he was a better person or a different person than he was. As a result of his Damascus Road experience, Paul found a new direction, a new sense of identity, and a whole new understanding of life, but he still had personal problems and he did not feel compelled to hide them. (Read II Corinthians.) Perhaps this is the crucial test of Christian freedom.

Christ can free us to reject even a religious façade and to accept the responsibility of an honest and open life. This may be why His words about freedom (John 8:32-36) were spoken to religious Pharisees rather than to "sinful" tax collectors. For all their religious posing, they were really "slaves to sin." They would not admit the truth about themselves, or about Jesus, and so they were not free.

Freedom is a gift which God gives His people when they accept His love for them in Jesus Christ. The authentic mark of the Christian style of life is that we live in God's freedom and transmit it to others.

Yet we find ourselves all too often living not as free men but as slaves. We fear to live freely, because it means risking rejection, ridicule, the loss of men's love. We pretend, posture, cover up, and live dishonestly. It is tragic that so many of us who have talked about God's unconditional love in Christ still continue to live closed lives before friends and fellow Christians. What is wrong?

It is as though we were marooned on a desert island and were given a boat. Though the boat be perfectly watertight and trustworthy, if we are afraid to launch out, to test it, we might as well have no boat at all. So also must our Christian freedom be tested, through confession, openness, and transparency.

We can begin by being totally honest with perhaps one other person; this is like shoving off from the shore for a trial run. Then, as we move on to honesty with the "significant others" in our lives, we discover that the boat will stand up in all weather, and we are free to leave the prison of the desert island.

As we confess to someone, we may fear that we will be rejected or betrayed. But as we let one member of the human race know what we're like, we let all people know, and somehow it doesn't matter how we're received. We have tested the fact that God has accepted us and we can live as those who fear no man. We are as free as the Apostle Paul to love men and to lose our lives for them.

What happens when we discover this gift of freedom?

A businessman spent years in fear that his wife would find out that he had once been unfaithful to her. Even though he now belonged to Christ, he lived as a slave, guilty and fearful, denied the gift of freedom. It was not until he told his wife about the past, risking his very marriage, that he discovered he had been free all along by an act of God's grace and forgiveness. It was not easy for his wife to forgive him, and it is a credit to her maturity and freedom that she did. The result was a great experience of new love.

A brilliant attorney lived for years under the onus of having cheated on his bar examination. There had been no question of his ability to pass, but his insecurity made him determined to get the highest mark in his group. Years after he became a Christian, he realized that he was still not free. So he wrote to the authorities and told them the whole story. He risked being disbarred, but found instead a very sympathetic group who understood and forgave. For this man, launching out into freedom meant that he no longer needed to fear the rejection of men, even professionally.

We need to be free to discover ourselves, rather than to justify ourselves. In his novel, *The Trial*, Franz Kafka describes a man who is going to be brought to trial by the state, but who is not told what the charges are against him. Free while awaiting trial, at first he tries desperately to pinpoint his crime, but finally he gives up and pathetically spends the rest of his life building a case to defend himself against the unknown charge. How aptly this describes the human predicament, even for many Christians!

In my own family life, I sometimes feel that my wife or children will reject me if they know that I have done something dishonest or untrue or unkind. I temporarily lose the gift of freedom as I cover up or justify myself. It's only as I tell my family what I am really like that I discover freedom again.

Honesty, then, can release us. How can we go on to transmit the gift of freedom to others?

Christ came to bring release to the captive. We can help others by our freedom from dependence on their love or approval. Here we need to take ourselves a lot less seriously and God's love a lot more seriously.

Freedom from other people's opinions has many dimensions. Several years ago I met a man, middle-aged, divorced, a gifted artist, who was looking for life and meaning. When he found the reality of Christ in a warm fellowship of people, he was free to stop giving dimes and quarters to vagrants on the street. Instead, he became involved with them and brought some of them to his home. This initiated some long, interesting, and demanding relationships.

He was also free to get involved in a costly way with social issues affecting his neighborhood. After two years as a solitary fighter for the rights of the oppressed, he began to see a change in a very difficult situation.

He became free of the need to impress his old pagan friends, even though he maintains his ties of friendship with them. More important, he is free not to have to impress his new Christian friends and do what they think "religious" people ought to do. Finally, he has become free to lose his life for others in specific ways. Presently, he has left a career in New York to go to Viet Nam to serve with the USO.

The whole world needs the freedom-with-responsibility that Jesus is giving to my friend. Albert Camus writes, "The aim of life can only be to increase the sum of freedom and responsibility to be found in every man and in the world. It cannot, under any circumstances, be to reduce or suppress that freedom, even temporarily."

The quality of freedom I have seen in my artist friend speaks of the style of life God wants to give to His people. "If the Son makes you free, you will be free indeed."

8. | THE GIFT OF DIALOGUE

DIALOGUE IS CONVERSATION between two or more persons. Too often prayer is a monologue in which we tell God about the things that are troubling us. When dialogue with God is discovered, a new relationship begins. It is the beginning of a life of adventure and partnership with God in the large and small affairs of everyday existence.

Henry B. Wright, a Yale professor, had this gift of dialogue. He also had a great concern for the well-being of friends, neighbors, and strangers. He tells of a time when he was distressed about a classmate who had ended up on skid row in New York City. After a weekend visit with his friend, Wright was on a train returning to Yale when God seemed to tell him to send the friend a gold watch with a certain inscription. Knowing that God often spoke in strange ways, he obeyed. The interest and concern expressed by that gift made such an impact on his friend that he stopped drinking and returned to a useful life.

When the professor saw the effect of his gift, he decided to send the same kind of gold watch with the same inscription to another alcoholic friend. This man promptly sold the watch to buy liquor!

God's guidance is unique. As we become involved with individuals, there are no patterns and no rules, but God can touch and reach people through us if we are sensitive and if we are in dialogue with Him.

The Bible records hundreds of conversations between God and individuals — kings, prophets, priests, soldiers, apostles, laymen, housewives, mothers. From the very first page of the Bible to the last, we find a record of God's dialogue with man. This record covers several thousand years of Biblical history.

God is the same today as He was in Biblical times, and there is no reason to believe that man is much different now than he was then. God wants us to talk with Him and He wants to talk with us. He talks to us about important things like our jobs, our marriages, our families, our neighbors, and our money, as well as about the things that seem unimportant. Every simple act or decision has tremendous potential consequences.

How does God speak to man in everyday life? Certainly by the "inner voice" which the Quakers stress. Sometimes this is called "the still small voice" in Scripture; or we may call it conscience. God also speaks through the Bible, through worship and meditation, through events, and through people, both friends and enemies. The initiative is God's in dialogue, and there are a hundred ways in which He can speak. Our role is to be receptive and expectant and to believe that God is speaking. A wise old friend of mine has said that when you seek God, you get guidance, but when you seek guidance, you get nothing. As we live out our lives in daily fellowship with God, He breaks through to us.

When does God speak? God is speaking all the time. He can speak when we most expect Him to, as in worship or in a quiet time alone early in the morning — or when we least expect Him to — perhaps in the events and circumstances of a busy day. The Bible tells of God speaking to Samuel in the temple. We know that Samuel was serving in the temple because God had spoken to his mother Hannah even before he was born. She was expecting God to speak while Samuel was not. But in both cases the initiative was God's and He communicated with both mother and son. (See I Samuel 1-3.)

When God speaks what does He say? We may expect it to be something "spiritual." God is a Spirit, but He is not "spiritual" as many of us mistakenly understand the word. When God appeared to Peter in prison in the form of an angel, He said only, "Quick! Get up. Do up your belt and put your shoes on. Now wrap your cloak around you and follow me." After the angel led Peter out of prison he disappeared (Acts 12:7-10, *New English Bible*). This is the extent of what God said to Peter at that time. How relevant and how "unspiritual." We are much more receptive to what God is saying when we realize that he often speaks most clearly in simple words about our present circumstances and relationships, and calls us to concrete action.

G. K. Chesterton, the great Roman Catholic layman, was once asked by an interviewer what book he would

like to have with him if he were marooned on a desert
island. As Chesterton began to consider this, the re-
porter made suggestions: the Bible? a volume of Shake-
speare? But Chesterton shook his head. "No. I would
like to have a manual on boatbuilding!"

With a manual on boatbuilding, Chesterton could
leave the island and buy a hundred Bibles and reach
countless men. God is more practical than any of us. He
is always concerned about our predicament and our circumstances, and He always has a relevant word.

The first twelve chapters of Genesis reveal three specific things that God says to man when man listens.

God asks Adam, "Where are you?" (Genesis 3). In
the creation story Adam and God are in fellowship and
dialogue until Adam sins. At the accustomed time of
meeting in the cool of the evening, Adam is hiding from
God. It is interesting to note that God comes seeking
man. He does not withdraw in shock because of man's
sin; rather, man conceals himself as a defense against
God. And God in His redemptive love asks the question,
"Where are you?"

God is still seeking us as He did Adam in all the hiding places we have devised. It is not God who is hiding
from man but man who is hiding from God. We might
paraphrase God's question to Adam in questions such
as: "Why are you so busy making money?" "Why are
you in so many clubs and activities, or in so much church
work?" "What are you hiding from in your business?"
"Why are you so mean to the people you love?" "Why
do you have to pretend you are different than you are?"

"Why do you wear the mask of superiority (or aloofness or indifference)?"

Certainly God already knows the answers to these questions, but when we can admit that our motives are devious and that our activities are often a cover-up, we can come out of our hiding places and stand naked before Him. It is at this point that a deep relationship based on God's love for us can be established.

A number of young couples in a church met to try to begin a depth relationship as Christians. For several hours they talked theology, philosophy, and politics. Finally a young mother of five broke in with, "You know, I sometimes feel I wasn't cut out to be a mother!" Honesty before God and her peers was the breakthrough the group needed. Others began to admit who they were, confessing their needs, their defeats, and their role-playing. The meeting broke up several hours later with laughter and tears and deep, honest prayer. As God asks the question, "Where are you?" we can answer honestly, either alone or in a group. In so doing we exercise faith and receive God's healing love.

At one point Jesus tells us to be like little children (Matthew 18:1-4). Of course, small children are far from perfect and just as self-centered as most adults. But they are usually more honest about their motives. Some years ago our young son Mark awoke from his nap to find his older brother drinking a large glass of grape juice. Mark wanted some, too, but his mother explained that the grape juice was all gone and poured him a glass of orange juice. Mark began to cry and insisted on grape juice. I was surprised to hear his usually competitive brother say, "Here, Mark, you can have my grape juice; I'll drink your orange juice."

Later when I drew Peter aside to tell him how proud I was of his unselfishness, he looked up at me amazed and said, "But Daddy, his glass was full and I had already drunk half of mine!" I understood then the virtue Jesus commended in little children. They are not unselfish, but they do not pretend to be something they are not. When we adults are as radically honest about ourselves as little children are, God can begin to heal us. God's questions about our motives and actions, past and present, hold the key to a life of faith. When Jesus stopped Paul on the Damascus Road, He asked, "Saul, why are you persecuting me?" Paul's maturity and readiness to respond is evidenced by the fact that he did not defend himself in any way. He was speechless and humble and broken. It was the beginning of a new life for him.

In the fourth chapter of Genesis we find another question typical of God's dialogue with man. Cain has just killed his brother in a jealous rage. God appears and asks, "Where is . . . your brother?" (Certainly God knew where Abel was, but Cain was given a chance to make the right kind of answer.) Instead of admitting he is a murderer, Cain dodges his responsibility, as so many of us do. He says, "How do I know? Am I my brother's keeper?" When we maintain our innocence or feign ignorance of our brother's predicament, we are in personal peril. Our honest answer to God and our honest answer before man indicates our faith in a God who loves us even when we are dead wrong. How different

Cain's life might have been if he had replied, "I murdered him. I was wrong. O God, forgive me!"

God is still asking us, "Where is your brother?" (or wife, or son, or mother, or employer, or neighbor). We can dodge God's loving questions with answers like these: "My marriage is a mess. I don't know what's the matter with my wife!" "I've done so much for my children and they're just not turning out right!" "What *more* do the Negroes want us to do for them?" "Who wouldn't cut corners on an employer like mine?"

In a touching autobiographical account,* Sarah Patton Boyle tells of facing God's questions in terms of her whole attitude as a southerner toward the Negro people. When she began to take responsibility, not just for her own actions but for the actions of all Americans in terms of their Negro brothers, new life and new love came to this extraordinary woman.

An executive with a top corporation in America was constantly at odds with his superior. When he had the courage to begin to reveal before God and his colleagues his attitude toward his employer, a new relationship began.

Many of us worry about a particular child who is failing in school or in some situation or relationship. When we can say in faith, "Maybe *I'm* the reason my son is failing," we find that God can not only change us but can begin to solve the problems of the person for whom we are concerned.

At a recent conference in Tennessee a minister said,

* *The Desegregated Heart* (New York: William Morrow & Co., Inc., 1962).

"I came to this conference feeling that I was serving the coldest church in the coldest denomination in Christendom. I was complaining to God about it just this morning in my prayers, and He said to me, 'Oh, John, I'm so sorry for you and the situation you're in. But if I can thaw you out and make you a loving, honest, and real person, maybe I can change your church and even part of your denomination through you.'" We all felt this was the start of something new not just for one minister but for countless people who will come under his influence in the years ahead.

We launch out in faith when we admit our guilt in our brother's predicament and begin to assume responsibility for him and for his well-being. The Biblical record of God's dialogue invites men to make honest answers to Him in our day. In this way we may be reconciled to Him and to each other.

In the twelfth chapter of Genesis we find God giving a simple directive which again is typical of His dialogue with man. He says to Abraham, "Go from your country and your kindred and your father's house to the land that I will show you." God is asking man to embark upon something that is new and threatening and frightening. To obey, no matter how difficult or hopeless the venture seems, is to act in faith. Jesus tells of two sons who were given a command by their father (Matthew 21:28-31). One said *yes* and did not do what he was asked. The other said *no* but later went and obeyed.

As God gives us a difficult command, we often instinctively say *no*, but upon reconsidering we may be obedient to it. It is not what we *say* but what we *do* that spells out our faith or lack of it.

Henry Drummond tells of a small child who asked his father, "What does God do all day long?" The man replied, "Why, He's just our Heavenly Father." The parent was not equipped or prepared to answer his child's profound question and to think of God as being more than a Heavenly Father. God is restless, creatively at work at all times. We must understand that God isn't only a Father and a Saviour and a living, comforting Spirit, but one who is at work, calling us to participation and partnership with Him in the re-creation of the world of men. Small children know their father as a father, but as they grow up they know him also as a merchant or carpenter or engineer — someone who is making his contribution to a busy world. As we mature as Christians, we realize that God is in action, creating, renewing, and redeeming, and that He calls us into action with Him day by day.

Some of my most vivid and grateful memories are of men and women who have had moral courage to respond to God in the twentieth century even as Abraham did almost three thousand years ago. I know a man who owned a bar. He became a Christian and felt God was saying, "Leave the liquor industry." He tried unsuccessfully for several years to find a buyer, but finally, in an act of moral courage, he gave away his business and opened a diner. Here is a modern Abraham who dared to leave the familiar and the secure and to venture into a new land of economic uncertainty.

An Air Force colonel believed he heard God say that

He had plans for the entire base under the colonel's command. With almost no background in the Christian faith, this officer began to act day by day under God's guidance, and eventually saw a change in both the morale and the performance of his unit.

A captain of industry heard God say to him, "Albert, there have been some real changes in your family life over the past few years. Now I mean to make some changes in this company, and you are the man through whom I intend to initiate them." By faith, the man is presently at work as a partner with God, trying to bring a new spiritual and ethical thrust into his business.

Many of us share the experience of Ananias (Acts 9: 10-19). One morning as he prayed, God told him to visit someone who was not only hostile to the Christian faith but who was responsible for the death and imprisonment of many of Ananias' Christian friends. Ananias argued with God, just as we do when we consider the terrific cost and risk of obedience. But finally he went to a street called Straight and looked up a man called Saul. The rest is history. Ananias found that God had prepared the way; his words and his presence were the means by which God's Spirit entered into Saul and made him the Apostle Paul.

Sometimes we are as reluctant as Ananias to obey God's guidance and to speak about God's love, even to our friends. But if we are obedient and in dialogue with God, He will guide us to those whom He has prepared.

God loves you and is speaking to you *now!* He is asking, "Where are you?" and, "Where is your brother?" and He is saying, as to Abraham, "Go!"

9. THE GIFT OF LOVE

A MIDWESTERN SCHOOLTEACHER tells of two small boys in his class who had the same last name but who were very different in appearance. When asked if they were brothers, one said, "Yes, but one of us is adopted, and I forget which one." To me, the parents of those two boys demonstrate unforgettably what real love is.

Man's need for love is universal. It is an established fact, for example, that babies in the first year of life may die or become permanently scarred simply for lack of love. Several years ago Psychiatrist René A. Spitz reported an extensive bit of research conducted in a foundling home. The ninety-one infants there had excellent food and care, yet twenty-seven of them died in their first year, and twenty-one were so impaired that they could only be classed as idiots. Although the food and the care were excellent, each nurse had ten children to supervise, so that each infant had only "one tenth of a mother." Dr. Spitz said that those who died "suffered a gradual breakdown under the stress, beginning with the loss of appetite and sleeplessness, and ending with inability to withstand even minor ailments. Love-starved, they were crippled in the battle for life."

One of the leaders in the emerging new school of psychiatry is Dr. William Glasser. In his book, *Reality Therapy*,* he affirms his belief that there is no such thing as mental illness. The deviant symptoms that we have come to classify as mental illness Dr. Glasser claims are the result of a frustration of two basic needs of life. Man needs to love and to be loved, and he needs to feel that he is worthwhile to himself and to others. If either of these needs is not being met, people tend to break down emotionally.

If we affirm the priesthood of all believers and the newly emerging lay ministry, we see that every Christian is called in some degree to be a therapist. To be effective, we must recognize the need for love in all people, and discern behind their many and varied requests a cry for this love. This certainly was one of Jesus' great secrets in dealing with people. He did not see a drunk or a prostitute or an uncouth fisherman. He saw persons desperately looking for love whose outward appearance would give no indication of what they really wanted and needed.

We are tested each day by people who make requests of us. When we are approached on the street by a dirty, foul-smelling drunk, we may react to the obviously unlovely and repulsive symptoms, or we may see behind the man's symptoms a child seeking the love he has never found.

A small boy kept asking his father to help him build

* New York: Harper & Row, Inc., 1965.

a clubhouse in the backyard. The father said he would, but each weekend he was involved in a business appointment, a golf date, some pressing homework, or a social engagement.

One day the little fellow was hit by a car and was taken to the hospital in critical condition. As his father stood at the bedside of his dying son, the last thing the little boy said with a smile was, "Well, Dad, I guess we'll never get to build our clubhouse." Of course, the boy didn't want a clubhouse as much as he wanted fellowship with his father.

In relating to people of any age, we need to be sensitive to what they are really saying to us. The Bible indicates that all men are motivated by this deep hunger for love. Christians are those who have experienced love and are in the process of sharing it with others.

Jesus, the incarnation of God the Father and His love, not only knows the most about the nature of God, but is also the great psychiatrist who most perfectly understands the nature of man. In the story of the prodigal son (Luke 15:11 ff.), His best-known and perhaps most profound parable, He tells about a certain father who had two sons. The story begins when the younger one asks his father for his share of the inheritance so that he can go out and make his fortune in the world. Most of us can identify with this young man in his search for money, things, popularity, sex, status, education, or merely escape from home and responsibilities. Man by nature seeks self-fulfillment. This may not be simply the kind of self-indulgence we find on skid row, but a more subtle self-indulgence through achievement in education, business, or society. We tend to prize material things and to see people as objects to be used in attaining them. Perhaps the most damning evidence of man's unredeemed nature is that he manipulates people to acquire things.

Consistent with this, we find in the parable that the turning point in the young man's life is not a "religious experience." In returning to the father, the son is not motivated by repentance, grief, remorse, or insight. He merely becomes disgusted with his own material and social lot in life. He is hungry and cold and lonely, and he dares to believe that his father may still love him enough to provide him with the simple necessities. Jesus realized that conversion may not be in any sense a *religious* experience, but rather a *common sense* experience. This is expressed flatly in the words, "He came to himself." The greatness of God's love is seen in His acceptance of man on these terms. Redemption for the prodigal also involved leaving the pigpen and starting the journey to his father's house. But the miracle of rebirth began at the very point of common sense.

I will always remember a student at Trinity College who began the Christian life with the confession that he was disgusted with the way he treated those he loved — his girl, his best friend, his parents. He turned his life over to God, simply to see if God could make him the kind of person he wanted to be with these people. At that point, the young man entered into an ever-expanding experience of newness through the Holy Spirit.

Jesus' parable might also be called the parable of the two sons. Many of us will see ourselves as the elder brother who stayed at home, worked hard, and was respectable in every way. But he was as lost as his younger brother, because he was working for wages and completely missing out on the marvelous gift of love and fellowship his father offered.

In too many marriages the husband or wife works for the approval of the other and misses the dynamic of real love. If our marriage is based on the idea, "I will do this for you if you will do that for me," we miss what love is all about.

I know a family, long considered the very "pillars of the church," in which mother, father, and all the children were active in church organizations, giving sacrificially of time, money, and leadership. One day the daughter was killed in an automobile accident while returning from a church conference. As far as I know, that family has not been inside the church since.

This tragic accident reveals the motivation behind so much religious life and church service. These people served God at great cost to themselves, hoping to put Him in their debt and to buy some kind of insurance against the misfortunes of life. When God did not "keep His part of the bargain," they stopped serving Him.

How many of us, like this family, or the elder brother in the parable, do the right things for the wrong reasons and miss the greatest gift that God has to give — the gift of His love!

Often the "elder brothers," "doing their duty," become the most unlovely people. They may not even have discovered the gift of human friendship seen in many pagans! In the parable the elder brother complains to his father that he has never received a fatted calf with which to entertain his friends. One writer has suggested that possibly he could have entertained his friends with a single mutton chop.

Fulton Sheen has said, "God prefers a loving sinner to a loveless saint." This can be misunderstood, but we all know what he means. In fact, we find the prodigal son much more lovable than his brother, even before his spiritual transformation.

In the same story, Jesus reveals the true nature of God's love. He describes the love that God has for us and challenges us to claim it. It is the kind of love with which we are to love one another as we become a part of God's new creation. It has been said that "some men by hating vice too much come to love men too little." We are not to hate evil so much as we are to love those caught in its grip.

Let us look at some of the characteristics of the father's love for his sons, as revealed in the story:

(1) *Love is permissive.* The father not only permits the son to go to his destruction in the far country, but actually gives him the resources which make it possible for him ultimately to destroy himself if he chooses. The cost of this kind of love is all too real to those of us who are parents. We tend to protect our children and keep them from being hurt, not always because we love them but because of the pain we suffer vicariously when they are hurt. To love our children permissively as they come of age is to experience a part of the very nature of the love of God.

Before I became a parent, I could never understand

God the Father. I understood Christ's suffering on our behalf, but the Father who gave His Son for us was incomprehensible. Now that I have children, I know that the greatest pain I have experienced over the years is to see them ignored, abused, or rejected by their companions. I have a totally new appreciation of God's love for me.

(2) *Love is ever forgiving.* In the parable, it is impossible to pinpoint the moment when the father forgives his son. The nature of God's love is to be forgiving all the time. When the son comes back asking for forgiveness, the father brushes the request aside and showers him with all that he needs. The real goal for Christians is to participate so freely and so fully in God's love that they do not even have to forgive, but act in a constantly forgiving way to all those who hurt them. When we understand this, we cease to beg for God's forgiveness. We accept His forgiveness and thank Him and praise Him. Even as we sin we are being forgiven. This is the devastating nature of the Cross.

(3) *Love is unconditional.* When the son returns to his father's house, there are no laws laid down for his behavior, no injunctions that he'd "better not make the same mistake again." The *New Yorker* magazine carried a cartoon some years ago that brilliantly expresses this powerful aspect of God's nature. It depicts a banquet hall full of servants and guests. The banquet table is loaded with a roast calf and trimmings. The father, about to carve the animal, turns to his younger son with a somewhat apprehensive look and says, "After all, Son, this *is* the fourth fatted calf!"

The nature of Christian freedom is that having returned to the father's house and having experienced his love, we are free once again, clothed and fed, to return to the far country if we choose. We stay close to the father only if we decide to do so. This unconditional love demonstrated by the father is frequently beyond most of us.

(4) *Love suffers.* The father never sent a CARE package to his son in the far country. He must have known where he was, for the elder brother reveals a detailed account of the younger brother's life in a discussion with his father in the fields. Yet the father allowed the son to go unfed and neglected, simply because he loved him too much to interfere in his life, and by interfering perhaps to keep him from "coming to himself."

This kind of love is costly. Several years ago we had a dog with a severe case of worms. The veterinarian prescribed some pills and told us not to give the dog food or water for forty-eight hours. During that period there was no way I could communicate to poor Kip that love kept me from feeding him or giving him water. The dog suffered during those hours, and so did I. In some small measure I learned what suffering love is like.

A doctor's wife was describing some vacation plans with her husband to a friend when the latter suddenly slapped her face and left the house. Struggling with her own pain and hurt, Lillian began to pray. God revealed to her that her friend was both threatened by, and jealous of, the quality of life that she and her husband shared. Later on, the woman called and apologized to Lillian, and began to admit the hurt and frustration of her own marriage. Out of our need we may slap God's face, but He continues to love us.

(5) *Love sacrifices.* When the prodigal son comes home, the father does not drag him off to a prayer meeting or sit around sentimentally embracing him. Instead, he provides food and clothes for the needy boy. He takes the part of the estate that is still left, and which rightfully belongs to him and to his elder son, and divides it with the younger son. How relevant God's love is! There is something profoundly "unspiritual" about the love of God as He demonstrates it to us daily. Christians need to be just this practical in demonstrating love to others.

During the 1966 subway strike in New York City, Dorothy Howard, the business manager of Faith at Work, spent three hours walking to and from work. There was only herself and one other girl to do the work of half a dozen people. I ride to the office by bus, and each day I would come in and give Dorothy some cheery word of faith and hope and assurance that God cared — but she seemed unresponsive and looked ever more harried and tired.

Then one morning my own frantic schedule seemed to overpower me, and losing all my faith in God's ability to provide, I went into Dorothy's office and confided that I didn't see how I could get my work done for the coming weeks. Amazingly enough she visibly brightened and immediately offered to pray for me. I found that when I shared my own needs with Dorothy and allowed her to minister to me, she found new strength for her own crushing situation. Chirpy optimism may be a terrible counterfeit for a real word of encouragement!

A half hour later Dorothy came into my office and offered the services of her one remaining secretary to help me with my work. I was overcome with the loving sacrifice I saw in this colleague — surely a reflection of God's love and care.

The dynamics of the Christian life are extremely simple, but not at all easy. They consist of three things: (1) repentance; (2) belief; (3) witness.

Repentance is nothing more than to "come to one's self." It is the moment of truth when we realize that our goals and our methods are false and that we are not truly happy or fulfilled. C. S. Lewis has said, "The hunger that the Lord has given you is the best gift you have." As we sit in the pigpen we realize that we have been looking in the wrong place for what is lasting and true and worthwhile. Repentance for the prodigal, however, did not mean merely a sense of regret, but enough disgust with his own condition to make him get up and leave the pigpen.

Belief for the Christian is not intellectual exercise, but rather a call to experiment. We test God's love to see whether He is a faithful father who will provide for all of our needs and take us back into His household again. Our whipping takes place in the far country, not in the household of God. We have been punished, and when we return to God, He lavishes upon us all those things we do not deserve but need so desperately. The root of sin is our refusal to be loved by God or to be part of His household, or to have fellowship with Him. Belief, or faith, means turning to God as He is revealed in Jesus Christ, and testing His nature.

A housewife in Connecticut was challenged by some friends in a small group to turn her life over to God. In all honesty she replied that this was impossible because her life was crammed with activities and obligations. Finally she agreed to an experiment. She would mark off one day on her calendar and she would give that day to God. When the fateful day came, she found she was unable to get out of bed because she felt ill. The doctor diagnosed her trouble as some very minor thing, but advised her to rest. Spending the day in bed, she realized that the thing she feared God would ask of her was even more "busyness." Instead, He had given her a day of rest to renew her body, mind, and spirit.

The third ingredient of the Christian dynamic is witnessing or passing on to others the love we have received from God. This, of course, includes sharing our substance, but it also means sharing ourselves. God's best gift to us is the gift of His love, and the best gift we have to offer to others is ourselves in deep and open fellowship. George Macdonald has said, "The love of our neighbor is the only door out of the dungeon of self."

At a men's retreat a truck driver told about the change Christ had made in his life, and I asked him to think of some specific way in which he was different. After a pause, he said, "Well, when I find somebody 'tailgating' my truck, I no longer drive on the shoulder of the road to kick up cinders on him." How simple but how profound is this understanding of what it means to love people in relevant and demonstrable ways.

All of us are on trial daily. We are being tested in every relationship as to whether we have received the gift of love from God and whether we are passing it on. While waiting for a plane at Chicago's O'Hare Field, I saw an elegantly dressed but obnoxious drunk careening through the lobby. It disgusted me that a man should be in that state at that hour. Later when the plane took off, I found myself seated by this very man. God gave me a second chance to love somebody whom I had despised earlier.

Most of us are surrounded by people with whom we have failed to share the gift of love. But God in His goodness usually gives us a second and a third and a seventy-seventh chance. How well we learn to love may determine the destiny of others. It certainly determines our own!

Last year in Canada I visited a friend whose life has been transformed by Christ. Roy left his job in the insurance business to serve on the staff of a rescue mission in a large city. As we chatted in his office, several of the mission's "clients" came in to report that old Charlie was lying in the snow outside. We went out to find a pathetic man, extremely drunk, in the grip of a heart attack. The difference Christ makes in a man's life was suddenly clear to me. The mission inmates could callously step over the man's body and simply report that old Charlie was out there again, but Roy rushed out to carry him in and minister to his physical needs.

Whether we live in a penthouse or on skid row, we are either the people who step over the bodies of those around us in our own quest for love, or we are those who go out and minister to the people who are dying on our doorstep for lack of it.

10. THE GIFT OF FELLOWSHIP

THE OTHER DAY the mailman brought my invitation to the annual reunion of the infantry division with which I served in World War II. I am always curious about these gatherings which, after twenty years, still attract men from all parts of the country who knew each other only a few brief months. I recognized none of the names on the invitation, and the actual friends anyone might meet at such an occasion would be few indeed. Then it occurred to me that perhaps for many this reunion offers a chance to be a part of a fellowship of men who once had a common purpose and a sense of destiny.

God has created everyone with a deep need for fellowship. Perhaps fellowship is the greatest gift He gives to us, next to the gift of Himself in Jesus Christ. Jesus said, "Where two or three are gathered together in my name, there am I in the midst of them" (Matthew 18:20, King James Version). This is what the Church is when it is truly the Church.

A Pittsburgh businessman began life "under new management" some years ago. This involved family devotions and, of course, church attendance, and at first his young children were bewildered. One night his youngest son was asked to wash his hands before coming to the table. When he protested that they were already clean, he was told, "Well, go and wash them anyway, because there are germs on them." "Germs and Jesus!" muttered the young lad. "Germs and Jesus! That's all you ever hear in this house, and you can't see either of them!"

Jesus may be as unreal to many of us as He was to this young boy. It is not enough to be told to follow Jesus. We must be a part of a fellowship that embodies His Spirit. Jesus knew that "two or three together" is essential if we are to experience authentic discipleship.

One of the most hopeful aspects of modern church life is the small group idea which promotes the rediscovery of fellowship. This is a fairly recent development. When I was a young man in Princeton Theological Seminary in the late forties and early fifties, the small group movement was unheard of but for a few prophetic voices. Among those who spoke and wrote much about this as a hope of the Church were Sam Shoemaker and Elton Trueblood. Men like these two were finally heard, and the Church is now discovering this authentic mark of New Testament Christianity.

But there is also despair and frustration in the small group movement currently sweeping every major denomination. Unfortunately, there is no magic in small groups. A church can organize experimental small groups, but New Testament fellowship does not necessarily result. People can continue to be strangers, meet-

ing on the periphery of life, without becoming a group
of people who have discovered the dynamic of "two or
three together."

There are many kinds of groups. Some are sterile and
dead and idea-centered, and some are groups of people
discovering each other, God, and the gift of fellowship.
Not long ago I walked into a home on a mountain over-
looking Phoenix, Arizona. Most of the twenty people
in the room knew only a few of the others. A meeting
was in progress, but with no agenda and no official
leader. Nevertheless, the reality of the fellowship was
electric. The host was a local surgeon. The guests were
varied: a clergyman from Los Angeles, a doctor and his
wife from Toronto, a retired school administrator, several
widows, widowers, and divorcees, a college professor
and his wife, and assorted businessmen and their wives.
When these people came together they found an im-
mediate awareness of and a receptivity to the mind and
the person of Christ, for separately they had discovered
the gift of fellowship.

On the other hand, groups may meet faithfully for
years yet never discover what this random group of
people found in their first hour together. Surely God
intends that the gift of fellowship be discovered by small
groups everywhere! Although a small group does not
guarantee fellowship, there can be no deep fellowship
unless there are small groups. One may never experience
intimate fellowship in a church of many hundreds or
several thousands unless there are small companies or
societies or cells. Most authentic times of renewal in
church history have been accompanied by this kind of

meeting, whether the class meeting of the Wesleyans in England, the Haystack prayer meetings of New England, or even the Monastic movement.

In our day psychiatry seems to be discovering the healing aspects of fellowship. A host of prophets, among them Mowrer, Glasser, and Szasz, are turning from counselor-centered therapy to the group concept. This is only one innovation, but there is ample evidence that people need to belong to a small company where they can know and be known by others before healing begins. The gift of fellowship is being discovered not only by the Church but by this band of experimenters who are opening new channels for the healing of individuals in our society.

Small group movements have been flourishing in recent years which have nothing directly to do with the Church or with psychiatry. The program of Alcoholics Anonymous is based on the principle that God's healing comes in an intimate sharing group of people who are fighting for wholeness for one another. The phenomenal success of Alcoholics Anonymous has spurred the growth of such groups as Narcotics Anonymous, Gamblers Anonymous, Neurotics and Schizophrenics Anonymous. There are even groups that might be labeled Overweight Anonymous. A report in the *New York Times* describes intensive control studies at Fort Dix, New Jersey, which reveal that encouragement from fellow sufferers is the greatest single aid to people who are trying to lose weight. Diets, medical aids, and many kinds of therapy have been used along with simple encouragement. Those who received encouragement from fellow sufferers had an overwhelmingly higher rate of weight loss.

This is not surprising when we understand that loneliness, separation, and isolation are at the core of much of the alcoholism, drug addiction, divorce, delinquency, and mental breakdown so common today. Many will remember Zangara, the man who made an attempt on the life of President Roosevelt years ago. An interview with him reported in the newspapers concluded with this question: "Do you belong to a church?" He replied, "No, no. I belong to nothing. I belong only to myself and I suffer." When a man belongs only to himself, he always suffers. He is subject to the most bizzare temptations, thoughts, and acts. This is why God wills us to belong to Him and to a few others who are trying to live out a life of obedience.

How can the groups we belong to be maximum in enabling people to discover this gift of fellowship? There are any number of excellent books on various group techniques and programs which give advice on how long the group should meet, when it should meet, or how much time should be devoted to Bible study, to prayer, and to fellowship. But I want to suggest five things that must take place within the context of the particular program your group has decided upon. These all have to do with *purpose,* for if the program is not serving the right purpose, the group cannot achieve the goal of fellowship.

A friend suggested entitling this chapter, "Scratch Where the Itch Is!" This sums up the whole purpose of a group. A group must be aware that people will bring to every meeting certain failures and needs and aspirations which come out of daily life. Unless the group allows the members to relate on this basis, fellowship is impossible.

(1) *Fellowship requires commitment to one another as firm as commitment to Christ.* When members of a group are detached observers, or believe they can teach one another from some superior position of knowledge or experience, fellowship is frustrated. It is not so difficult to commit ourselves to Christ, for we know that He is always reliable and trustworthy. But to obey His commandment and to love one another as He has loved us requires all the faith a man has. Perhaps the hardest thing we are asked to do is to give ourselves unreservedly to another person or to a few other persons. We know that people are not always trustworthy. It should be said at the beginning of a group meeting that each person there is entrusting himself, his fortune, his reputation, and his security to the others in the expectation that God will begin to heal and guide.

Bill Milliken lives and works on the Lower East Side of New York City. God has done amazing things through his ministry in one of our nation's neediest areas. Sociologists, psychologists, and theologians have often failed to achieve the kind of success with people which Bill has experienced. His secret is simple. He has identified with the people there! He moved from the suburbs of Pittsburgh into a tenement apartment and shared the life of his new neighbors. In the early years they stole from him (and some still do), ignored him, and ridiculed him, hoping that he would leave. But when they discovered that Bill had cast his lot with them, they began to trust him. He brought them the gift of fellowship, and now there is a whole company of young people and adults on the Lower East Side who are living in New Testament fellowship, claiming life in Christ and offering this life to their contemporaries. The ingredient is just as essential for the small group in suburbia.

A corresponding experiment in the Westminster Presbyterian Church of Madison, Wisconsin, has resulted in a number of members meeting weekly with prisoners in a local state penitentiary. Under the guidance of the prison chaplain, "Oz" Anderson, they have been able to bring the gift of fellowship to a great number of prisoners. They are in no way condescending, nor do they come as experts giving advice. They have shared their lives as equals with the prisoners and have discovered that they are all brothers. As some men are released from prison, they find a warm welcome from their friends in Madison who are committed to the prisoners not only for the duration of their sentences but also for the difficult weeks and years of readjustment to life on the outside. Commitment to one another is at the very heart of this unique experiment, which has attracted the attention of penal experts across the country.

(2) *True fellowship consists of honesty to the point of vulnerability.* This simply means that as people come together they need to talk about their failures, both past and present. Most of us shy away from this. We want to be honest categorically and generally — but not specifically. It's easy to say that we are sinners, but it is extremely costly to let a group know where we fail our

families, friends, society, and ourselves. This is vulnerability.

I have been told that if you stop overnight with the mountaineers in the South, hospitality will be extended even if you are a stranger. Food and lodging will be offered graciously. But by tradition, if you bring a loaded gun into the house, you awaken to find your gun broken open and the cartridges lined up beside it. This is a mountaineer's way of saying that friendship is costly, and to receive it you must put yourself at the other's mercy. There is a lesson here for any small group.

Paul Tournier, the Swiss psychiatrist, discovered a new kind of counseling which exemplifies this relationship. In all of his recent books Tournier indicates that when he is personally vulnerable with his patients and lets them know something of his own failures, healing takes place. When he is merely "professional," he fails to see the same results.

In the same way, we who are church leaders must begin a group by admitting our own needs and aspirations. If we're there to "help other people," or as part of some new program, we are almost certain to fail.

(3) *A group must have relevance to the world in which the members live.* It is easy to form a study group to discuss Biblical theology, philosophy, and theoretical Christian ethics. But Jesus Christ is the great eternal contemporary. If His Spirit is present in a group, we must examine the personal life of each member and the social structures surrounding the group corporately in the light of commitment to Him.

In Pittsburgh, Pennsylvania, under the general name

of The Pittsburgh Experiment, groups of men and women are involved in this kind of relevant ministry. Hundreds of people from all walks of life meet at various hours of the day in factories, offices, schools, and churches. But the common ministry of these groups living in fellowship with each other, studying the Bible, and praying together is their concern for the people around them. Each group is involved not only with the personal problems of individuals, but with problems of labor and management, the unemployed, alcoholics, prisoners, delinquents, the poverty-stricken. They are discovering that Jesus Christ is in the world, and they meet Him when they come into vital contact with the world and discover His will and plan for meeting the world's needs.

(4) *True fellowship involves accountability to one another.* To be the authentic body of Christ, we must take responsibility for each other. People need to "report in" each week and tell about the experiment of Christian living in their own lives. Fellowship necessitates fighting for the other person's best. This does *not* mean telling others in the group what they should do, but when an individual expresses a conviction that he feels is of God for his own life, the rest of the group should hold him to it.

In a church which my wife and I served, we were in such a group. At a certain meeting my wife "reported in" that in her devotional time that week God seemed to be asking her to write letters of apology to two women with whom she had previously worked. Each week thereafter, someone would ask Hazel whether she had written those letters. With growing exasperation, she had to say no. Months went by before she got around to writing the letters, but when she did the results were beyond expectation and the relationships were healed. Apart from the group which held my wife to God's best for her, she might not have taken those steps to health and wholeness.

We need to be careful not to give advice to one another. Rather, as we share our own experiences, God can speak to another person and reveal answers for his life.

At a conference in the Pocono Mountains, a teacher from an inner-city school in the East told of her disappointment with integration. Before her school was integrated, she had greatly enjoyed teaching. But now, with many underprivileged Negroes in the student body, she found strife and turmoil and misunderstanding, and she wanted to change jobs.

When it was her turn, another member of the group, a Negro mother living in a similar inner-city environment, told of *her* disappointment with an integrated school. One of her children was in the eighth grade and still could not read or write properly. She felt this was because all the better teachers had moved out when the school was integrated and the new teachers were not competent.

At the closing meeting of that group, the white teacher revealed that God had spoken to her through the Negro mother, and she had decided to stay in her school. This is how God convicts His people through one another when there is true fellowship.

(5) *In fellowship, it is not enough to be honest about our sins, past and present. If we are to share life together, we must learn to express our dreams and aspirations.* This may be where we are most vulnerable. We fear that our desire to change jobs or go back to school or begin a new business or a new venture will be laughed at — or we feel we are being presumptuous. But when we are committed to one another, we can tell the people who have begun to know us about our hopes and dreams. Then we open ourselves to God's guidance through group "corrective." Others who know us may be able to confirm our dreams as authentic. I have seen people begin new jobs or launch out in some new project simply because the group has affirmed that a long-standing dream most certainly sounds "of God." Their encouragement to go ahead may mean that they must stand with the person in the financial and social risks involved. It is in this area that the prophetic nature of a group can best be exercised.

To discover the reality of Christian fellowship is to enter an exciting new life. When we walk into this dimension of "two or three together," we can no longer go back to the old solitary kind of discipleship that has all too often characterized the Church. One Canadian woman who experienced the release that comes from moving out of isolation into belonging began thirty small groups in her home church in the space of a few months. Her own enthusiasm brought people together to discover what she had found.

Today the Church is finding that part of God's strategy for renewal lies in the small group discovery of the gift of fellowship. A few years after the close of World War II a pastor in the heart of Frankfurt told how his church had been destroyed by bombs. But he said, "I am in no hurry to rebuild. Since there is no room in the parish where more than twenty people can meet, they are coming in small groups for prayer and Bible study. I used to climb into the pulpit and talk to a crowd. Now I am getting very close to people in their little meetings. There is more real religion than we had in a building."

Some years ago Billy Graham was asked what he would do if he were to become the pastor of a large church in a principal city. His answer, in part, was, "I think one of the first things I would do would be to get a small group of eight or ten or twelve men around me who would meet a few hours a week and pay the price! It would cost them something in time and effort. I would share with them everything I have, over a period of a couple of years. Then I would actually have twelve ministers among the laymen, who in turn could take eight or ten or twelve more and teach them." Christ Himself set the pattern. He spent most of His time with twelve men — with eternal results.

In one of the great documents of our time, the late Dr. John Heuss, rector of Trinity Episcopal Church in the heart of the Wall Street area of New York City, described the true function of a parish. This is how he saw the strategy of renewal: "It is a growing conviction of mine that no parish can fulfill its true function unless there is at the very center of its leadership life a small community of quietly fanatic, changed, and truly converted Christians. The trouble with most parishes is that nobody, including the rector, is really greatly changed; but even where there is a devoted, self-sacrificing priest at the heart of the fellowship, not much will happen until there is a community of changed men and women."

On every side there are abundant signs of hope. Renewal is coming to Christ's Church in our day as we discover, in the small group movement and elsewhere, the gift of fellowship.